Freda

Love You
So much!

Mary

-JD

HARVESTING
HOPE

MARY JO BROWN

WESTBOW
PRESS®
A DIVISION OF THOMAS NELSON
& ZONDERVAN

Copyright © 2017 Mary Jo Brown.

All rights reserved. No part of this book may be used or reproduced by any means, graphic, electronic, or mechanical, including photocopying, recording, taping or by any information storage retrieval system without the written permission of the author except in the case of brief quotations embodied in critical articles and reviews.

Scripture quotations marked (NIV) are taken from the Holy Bible, New International Version®, NIV®. Copyright © 1973, 1978, 1984, 2011 by Biblica, Inc.™ Used by permission of Zondervan. All rights reserved worldwide. www.zondervan.com The "NIV" and "New International Version" are trademarks registered in the United States Patent and Trademark Office by Biblica, Inc.™

Scripture taken from the New King James Version®. Copyright © 1982 by Thomas Nelson. Used by permission. All rights reserved.

This book is a work of non-fiction. Unless otherwise noted, the author and the publisher make no explicit guarantees as to the accuracy of the information contained in this book and in some cases, names of people and places have been altered to protect their privacy.

WestBow Press books may be ordered through booksellers or by contacting:

WestBow Press
A Division of Thomas Nelson & Zondervan
1663 Liberty Drive
Bloomington, IN 47403
www.westbowpress.com
1 (866) 928-1240

Because of the dynamic nature of the Internet, any web addresses or links contained in this book may have changed since publication and may no longer be valid. The views expressed in this work are solely those of the author and do not necessarily reflect the views of the publisher, and the publisher hereby disclaims any responsibility for them.

Any people depicted in stock imagery provided by Thinkstock are models, and such images are being used for illustrative purposes only. Certain stock imagery © Thinkstock.

ISBN: 978-1-5127-8011-6 (sc)
ISBN: 978-1-5127-8013-0 (hc)
ISBN: 978-1-5127-8012-3 (e)

Library of Congress Control Number: 2017904247

Print information available on the last page.

WestBow Press rev. date: 04/03/2017

Dedicated to all who need hope.

The righteous cry out, and the Lord hears them; he delivers them from all their troubles. The Lord is close to the brokenhearted and saves those who are crushed in spirit. A righteous man may have many troubles, but the Lord delivers him from them all; he protects all his bones; not one of them will be broken.

—Psalm 34:17–20 (NIV)

CONTENTS

Acknowledgments ix
Introduction xi

1. As the Twig Is Bent 1
2. Abandoned 11
3. Stepmother Rules 20
4. The Darkest Years 33
5. Life with Mother 67
6. Reunion 78
7. Colorful Colorado 91
8. What I am Doing Now? 104

Epilogue 107
About the Author 115

ACKNOWLEDGMENTS

This book was written in loving memory of my grandma and for my two sisters and brother and my friend Molly, a writer who encouraged me to tell our story. But most of all, it is written to honor God our Father who sent His only Son, Jesus Christ, to die for our sins. God gave to us the wisdom and strength to endure the trauma described in this book.

This story is true, although I've changed names and dates to protect the privacy of family members. "Mary Jo Brown" is an assumed name, as are the names of my family members. My goal is to put the spotlight on Jesus—the perfect and holy One.

INTRODUCTION

Kansas is a beautiful state. Its corn reaches for the sky and the wheat fields glitter like gold. I love to see the fields flourishing: "First the blade, then the ear, after that, the full corn in the ear," as the scriptures say.

Unfortunately, not every citizen in the Wheat State can match our countryside in beauty. Cursed by sin and struggling to "give truth a luster and make wisdom smile," (Source of this quote is Comp. H.B. Lighthizer of the Grand Chapter of California) my family suffered from the harmful influence of alcohol and bore the consequences of selfish greed. This is my personal story of how my sisters, brother, and I were able to survive some difficult times growing up. By banding together, we put our hands in the Savior's strong grip and hung on hard.

My mother grew up in a small Kansas town as the oldest of eight. Grandpa and Grandma Patterson owned approximately 160 acres, and my grandfather worked the farm. Growing up, my mother's family was reasonably steady until Grandpa's boozing habits turned him violent and abusive. The wrath of the alcoholic husband and father fell most frequently on his eldest daughter.

Not surprisingly, when my mother was seventeen, she married Loy Brown, who lived on a neighboring farm. My father, Loy Brown, was given the enormous gift of five hundred acres of land at the age of eighteen so that his prosperity would be assured. That gift represented a lot of potential wealth in those days. Loy wanted to have many sons who could work his land, but God gave him three girls before he would get his only son.

"I married young to escape all the violence and oppression," my mother told me many times. However, her simple "I do" on her wedding day led to a lifetime of regret and anger. By the grace of God, we kids eventually found hope in the promises of our Savior after Grandma Brown led each of us to repeat the sinner's prayer of repentance and ask for divine help.

Our childhood legacy needed the sunshine of God's love and the comfort of His abundant grace. Nothing says it better than the promise written in Latin that heralds the Lord's righteous kingdom to come: *Christo et regna ejus!* Some of us took a long time getting there.

Chapter 1

AS THE TWIG IS BENT

From birth I was cast upon you: from my mother's womb you have been my God. Do not be far from me, for trouble is near and there is no one to help.

—Psalm 22:10–11 (NIV)

There are fewer people living on the 82,276 square miles of the entire state of Kansas than there are in each of America's three largest cities, so there's plenty of room for everybody. I never got tired of watching the fields sprout and grow green after the blizzards of winter, and my home state of Kansas represents to me everything that is noble and good in the development of our country. But it holds its share of agony and painful memories for me as well. Both of my parents were very hard workers. Each year, Mom tended large gardens and canned fruit and vegetables in such large quantities that many of our winter meals came totally from her preserves. When the weather was good, Dad worked in the fields from sunup to sundown. In addition to her gardening, Mom was an excellent seamstress and made dresses for Freda May, Anna Kate, and me. She patched Bobby Dean's britches and made him his shirts for outdoors.

Dad played parlor games with us in the evenings when we were small, but as we grew older, he had less time to spend with us.

When he wasn't working in the fields, he was watching the news and commenting on national and state issues and debates. He pored over maps, making us memorize every county in Kansas, and he recounted political events from Kansas City to Mount Sunflower (the highest point in Kansas on the Colorado border).

Grandpa and Grandma Brown, our paternal grandparents, were a big influence on our entire family. Grandpa served during the Roosevelt era as postmaster for our town, and Grandma delivered mail as a postal carrier. They did not lose their jobs during the Depression. Toward the end of the Depression, they bought land for pennies per acre with their savings. Since they were both well-liked in the community, many people would sell their land to them for a good price in order to keep their credit good rather than have to foreclose on their farms. Grandpa and Grandma did not want to take advantage of them and were very upset about the Depression and the devastation it brought to the entire country.

"It changed me forever," Grandma said. "These hard times taught me that you can have all the wealth in the world and lose it in no time."

Grandpa and Grandma Brown had two sons—our father, Loy, and his brother, Hank Ray, who was the only one to attend college. While Hank was at college, he met a girl who later left him and broke his heart. After that time, Uncle Hank Ray never worked at a job or made a living in any way. He lived off his inheritance of five hundred acres of land given to him when he was eighteen, and he slowly sold it off until there was nothing left.

Good-bye to the Nearest and Dearest

Grandpa Brown was a gentle man. He loved to play games with my sisters and me. He took time to listen to our little-girl issues and offered comfort if we were disappointed about something. I thought he would be a part of our family forever.

But one night in 1958, Uncle Hank Ray began to argue with Grandpa. Their voices grew louder and louder. Everybody in the house stopped what they were doing. It was terrible. We children were quickly hustled off to bed. It was the last time we saw Grandpa. The house became eerily quiet that night. Sometime in the darkest hours before dawn, Grandpa died of a heart attack.

With our peacemaker gone, Dad and Mother began to argue. They would disagree about small issues at first. Later they would scream verbal abuse at each other. At this time, two of Mother's brothers, Uncle Bill and Uncle Carl, for some unknown reason stopped living with Grandmother Patterson, so they were sent to live with us. We welcomed them eagerly because we had fun playing games with them. We learned from everybody, even from those whose lives were erratic and whose personalities were a bit different.

Grandpa Patterson, at least half Cherokee Indian, taught us, "When you give someone your word, you must keep it. This reflects your worth. People who don't keep their word have no self-worth. You just can't trust them."

But beyond his honor and hard work, Grandpa Patterson had a bad side—caused by his drinking. The good side consisted of his honor and hard work; the bad side came with the change that liquor made inside him. I was so impressed by Grandpa's rock-solid honesty that I determined I would always keep my word too—because "it is the right thing to do."

Farm Life, Kansas Style

I'm the middle daughter in the feminine trio of the Browns. My older sister, Freda May, has brown eyes and medium-brown hair that is thick, with tight, natural curls. Freda May and I fought about something every day, but I was stronger and would beat her up if she got too bossy. Freda May would gladly work at chores to help anyone. Grandma Brown had some pigs that needed care. Freda May fed and watered those pigs on our farm. She took care of them asking for no reward. When Grandma gave them to her, my younger sister and I learned a valuable lesson: sometimes a thoughtful, caring heart is rewarded when nothing is expected. Freda May is the most loving sister anyone could have.

Anna Kate is the youngest of the Brown sisters. She's beautiful, with long, black hair and brown eyes. I don't mean just *beautiful*, I mean *gorgeous*. Always nervous about the issues of life, of right and wrong, and of honesty and dishonesty, she let the littlest things bother her. Growth and maturity did not come easily for Anna Kate. She hated fighting and all physical violence. Her body was small and delicate—just what you'd expect from a beautiful little girl. Though she tried valiantly, she could not defend herself in a fight. If someone did her a favor, she never forgot it.

And Baby Makes Four

Our brother, Bobby Dean, was born last. He had brown hair and brown eyes. Dad loved Bobby Dean in a special way. When I was younger, Bobby Dean was my best friend. As a tomboy, I enjoyed playing his games, but as he grew older, our brother spent almost all his time with Dad out in the barn or in the fields with tractors, combines, and plows.

At the age of three, Freda May started running away from home. To this day, nobody quite knows why. Today she explains simply with a shrug, "Something must have been wrong in my little-girl world." There was a lot of that, so she's probably right. You have to hand it to a little tot of three years who discerned trouble at home and wanted to get away. She would spend a good portion of her time at Grandma Brown's house—a safe haven for all of us, as you'll see.

One night Freda May asked if she could go to Grandma's house, but our parents forbade it. "Call Grandma," Freda May insisted. "She wants me to come." She pulled rank by appealing to a higher power.

"The phones don't work after ten o'clock," Mother explained, hoping to settle her down. This only made Freda May cry harder and jump up and down on the bed. Mother finally relented and placed a call at 10:30. Grandma came immediately and took Freda May home with her. These visits increased until Freda May was spending more time with Grandma than she was at home. Mother didn't seem to care.

One day at our house while playing hide and seek, Mother found Anna Kate and me, but not Freda May. We figured she had run off to Grandma's house again. When she came out of hiding, everyone was gone. She wondered if the world had come to an end. Had the end of the world come, and had she missed it?

Our father built us a wooden playhouse in a tree. As soon as he pounded the last nail, we three girls went straight up there to bake mud pies. When they were done, we offered some to Anna Kate. "Taste our specialty pie," we urged her.

I pressed the pie toward her, smiling winsomely. Anna Kate took it. She almost ate it, but she kept looking at us and suspected something. Suddenly, Freda May and I couldn't hold back our laughter any longer. Holding our stomachs, we roared with glee. Anna Kate just stared at us blankly. She didn't know what was so funny. That made Freda May and me laugh even harder.

The Kansas Twisters

Days in the playhouse ended with tornado warnings in the news that summer of 1959. We watched angry black clouds boil up outside, sometimes with a funnel hanging below them, sucking up the countryside. This was the part you didn't want to see. What would happen next? To be safe, we all headed for the storm cellar with lanterns and some bedding. All night long the wind howled. In the morning we looked out to see our playhouse upside down, broken to pieces. Despite our pleading, Dad would not fix it. I don't know why. He hauled it off to the ditch. Times were just too hard to begin making another playhouse, my father must have reasoned.

Dad wasn't much for presents. Each time Christmas came around, Dad wanted to skip the celebration, but that never happened. Thanks to money from Grandma Brown for presents, we all had something new to wear and something fun to play with. Dad would buy presents for only one child—Bobby Dean. But we had fun in other ways.

Grandma bought fifty chicks every spring. She taught us how to take care of them every day. I said, "I'll feed them when I feel like it." Grandma said, "They need to be watered and fed every morning and night." I forgot to feed and water them for a couple of days, and several of the chicks died. Grandma told me, "Anything you don't value and take care of, you will lose sooner or later." My favorite chick died, and I was devastated. I told Grandma that I would take it back. Grandma said, "There is no taking it back. You take care of them so they live, or you don't and they die." I never missed feeding and watering them again. Later that month, a friend from wanted me to go immediately to a birthday she was having after school. I told her that I had to feed and water the chickens. She said, "Let's go now. I need to get home and get ready." I told her, "I'm not letting the chickens go hungry, so either wait fifteen minutes or go without me. I'm not leaving without feeding them." She said that I was the most stubborn person she had even met. She finally said, "Hurry up, and I'll wait." I fed and watered the chickens, and then I asked Grandma if I could go to the party. I didn't know that Grandma Brown had been listening and was pleased that I was learning responsibilities, so she quickly said, "Yes, but be back by nine o'clock."

Every late summer when the chickens were full grown, it came time to chop their heads off and watch them flop around. Then we would dip each one in boiling water until the feathers loosened. Then all of us yanked the feathers off. After that, Grandma would start a fire and singe off all the hair.

I told Grandma that I didn't want to see their heads cut off since I had grown fond of them. Grandma said, "Mary Jo, it might have been best for you to lose your favorite chick months ago, or losing her now would be really hard." I said "Either way is hard, Grandma. I think I have a hard time letting go of the ones I love." Grandma said, "It will cause you extreme pain at times in your life, but I so admire it."

Mother cut open the backs between the legs and took out the entrails, carefully separating the giblets (heart, liver, and gizzard) to use later in gravy. We cut off their yellow feet, washed the chickens, and placed each in heavy white paper for the freezer.

The Fruit of Carelessness

One day Mother and Grandma Brown went shopping in town. They bought groceries and a carnival kit. Mom put the kit on a high shelf in her bedroom closet so it would be opened later. But Freda May and I couldn't wait. We wanted to see what a carnival kit looked like, so Freda May dragged an old, discarded aquarium into the closet and positioned it as a stool. Just as we got the aquarium to the bed, Anna Kate came in the room. Fred May's goal was to use it to reach the top shelf. She carefully placed the aquarium on its side, stepped on it, and reached eagerly for the top shelf. Cracckkkk! Freda May came tumbling down just like Jack and Jill. She looked at the blood spurting from her leg, felt a stab of pain, and screamed. So did we. I don't think I'd even seen that much blood appear so quickly. Anna Kate ran outside and hollered to Grandma, who had just pulled into the driveway, "Freda May cut her leg off!" she cried hysterically.

Frantically, Grandma rushed in and stretched her out on the linoleum floor. She carefully cleaned Freda May's wounds, and then she applied salve before bandaging them. Three deep gashes kept Freda May off that leg for a while. She had no stitches because neither Grandma nor Dad believed doctors could help her that much. Freda May received a flaxseed poultice to put on the gashes, but there were no shots. Slowly, my sister's wound healed, and she became her spunky self again.

It seemed as if while Freda May was getting better, Anna Kate was getting worse. Anna Kate was having trouble breathing and was sickly most of the time. Swelling went from her throat all the way up to her ears. Her tonsils, too, had become badly infected. She was getting worse by the day, gasping for breath. She couldn't eat any food and ran a constant fever. Finally, Mom stepped in and took Anna Kate to the doctor. He stated that my sister would need to have her tonsils removed that week. Mother decided on a package deal. All three of us had our tonsils removed. I threw up a lot but recovered more quickly than either Anna Kate or Freda May. Whenever we developed a fever, Grandma would give us her surefire remedy—enemas—to reduce the high temperatures.

Mother Makes Plans without Us

In the early fifties, we noticed that Mom was becoming increasingly unhappy with each passing day. Fighting between our parents became more frequent as their relationship deteriorated.

Although we didn't know it, Mother began to make plans to leave Dad. It seems that her decision to leave did not consider who would be most affected in her decision, including what her move would do to us kids or her brothers. In January 1960, Mom went out to a bar with her girlfriend Gert. She took us kids with her to get out of the house. Mom met a man in a bar who set her heart to beating a little faster. She fancied herself in love with him and made plans to leave Dad. At that point it was only a matter of time before Mom would be out of our lives for good. Mom's change in behavior was too painful for us to comprehend, so we kept playing games, reading, working, and letting life go by.

Looking back, we were resilient. Even faced with the inevitable destruction of our home as we knew it, we looked for ways to entertain ourselves. Once a week, our neighbors stretched a sheet between two poles and set up a projector so our whole town could come and watch a movie. Some of the movies were scary, with monsters eating people and earthquakes shaking down skyscrapers. During a movie with a dragon coming after a beautiful damsel tied to poles, Anna Kate mentioned Mom had disappeared and was looking around for her. The dragon was getting closer to the damsel, and I said, "Who cares? She's going to be goner if someone doesn't get to her fast! Look! The dragon has fire coming out his mouth! Holy cow!" The movie was so good, and after all, Mom was still there at the end of the movie.

Mom promised Freda May she would take her to a dance as a present for her ninth birthday. At first, Dad said a firm no. He would not go either. Eventually Dad relented and Mom took Freda May to a dance on Saturday night. Freda May had a new dress and pretty shoes to go with it, and she looked great.

Freda May loved hearing the music and watching the dancers swirl around the floor. Her great desire was to be asked to dance. Suddenly she realized that Mom was not with her. "Where's Mom?" she asked. Gert didn't answer. She only looked toward her car outside in the parking lot. Its windows were all steamed up. Gert suggested they go inside to the dance floor. Eventually Mom came looking for them. She wanted to go home immediately. Freda May lost her chance to dance in her new dress. She was devastated.

Mom's two brothers had been living with us for two years now. Bill, the older one, worked for wages on our farm and was paid by Dad; the younger one, Carl, went to school with us. Bill went to high school in another town.

By the spring of 1960, Mom had made up her mind to leave Dad, which also meant that she was leaving her children and her two brothers. One morning, Mom packed her clothes and some other items. Some man in a car drove up the driveway to pick up Mom, Anna Kate, and Bobby Dean. Freda May and I had left early in the morning to catch the bus for school. They drove to Grandma Brown's home. Mom went into the house with Anna Kate and Bobby Dean and told Grandma Brown that she was leaving. She had brought Anna Kate and Bobby Dean for Grandma to take care of.

"Do you know what you're doing?" Grandma asked her with tears running down her cheeks.

"Yes," Mom replied. "And I won't be back."

Uncle Bill watched Mother pack her suitcases and carry them to the car of a man who had come for her. Dad came running in from the field. He seemed crazed with grief. "Stop her!" he ordered Bill just as she drove away. "Bring her back!"

Uncle Bill shook his head as he jumped into our car and raced down the road after Mom and the man who had stolen her love.

Uncle Bill couldn't keep up with them, but he stayed on their trail, which led to a small town about twenty miles away. He located their car, parked in front of a house, and got out of the car and knocked on the front door. The door flew open and there stood an angry man with a gun pointed at Uncle Bill.

"I-I'd like to talk to my sister," Uncle Bill stammered.

"You ain't talkin' to nobody," the stranger growled. "Leave now or you'll die." He raised the gun for emphasis.

Fearful and trembling, Uncle Bill turned and ran to his car. He drove back to our house and reported his failure. Dad pulled out a knife and raised his eyebrows. "I have the power now," he said as he threatened Uncle Bill.

Uncle Hank Ray suddenly appeared out of nowhere and ordered Uncle Bill to get his things and get out. He'd hold Dad off. Uncle Bill ran to find Uncle Carl. They collected their things and tore off down the road. They were too frightened to return to Grandma Patterson's house because they knew they would not be welcome there either. They lived together in Uncle Bill's car for a while and then both men went to live with their other sister for a while. This lonely and desperate time continued for several years.

ABANDONED

> The Lord is close to the brokenhearted and saves those who are crushed in spirit. A righteous man may have many troubles but the Lord delivers him from them all; he protects all his bones, not one of them will be broken.
>
> —Psalm 34:18:20 (NIV)

1960–1963

Freda May and I arrived home on the school bus as usual on the afternoon Mom left us never suspecting that our lives were going to change drastically. Grandma Brown was at our house. We thought little of it because she visited frequently. As we walked into the house, Grandma had the saddest face I have ever seen, and she motioned for Freda May and me to come to her side. "Your mother has left," she said.

"You're lying!" I blurted out. "Our mother would never leave us."

"I'm sorry, sweetheart," Grandma whispered, "but yes, she has left."

Just then, Freda May came into the room with a puzzled look on her face. "Mom must have left," she said. "I can't find her anywhere."

I put my hands on my hips and cried, "Say that again, and I'll beat you to a pulp. Mom would not just leave like this!" I wanted to stop breathing.

Grandma Brown began to cry. I'd never seen her cry like that. I thought I was going to choke to death from my own grief, surprise, and anger. The pain of abandonment is excruciating. It leaves an ugly mark on anyone it happens to. Naturally, we blamed ourselves. It must have been something we did to make our mother walk out on us. Freda May and Anna Kate became depressed, and it was the worst time of our lives.

Our New Home

Grandma Brown gathered us up in her loving arms and took us all to her house for the night because Dad had lost his senses. "Either take the kids," he told Grandmother, "or they'll have to go to an orphanage."

Dad was so distraught in his anguish that he shut off the heat in the house that night in freezing temperatures. By midnight he had slipped into a coma. Fortunately, Uncle Hank Ray went over to the house late that night to check up on his brother. He found Loy unconscious, and he dragged him into his car and brought him back to Grandma's house where we were staying.

Freda May prayed, "Please, Lord, don't take my daddy, too."

In our new home at Grandma's house, we had plenty of woods and acres of pastureland to explore. Grandma taught us how to do chores, how to sew, cook, and clean the house. When we behaved badly, Grandma would try to hit our legs with the branches of bushes that she called a switch. It would really sting if it hit your leg. We would run as fast as we could, and Grandma would have a hard time getting our legs.

In the woods, we found mushrooms in the spring and played on the vines pretending to be like Tarzan. Some people told us the thick woods behind us were haunted. That just made them more fun and exciting.

Grandma Brown, who loved us unconditionally, devoted herself to us totally. As we girls grew taller and stronger, we were able to help more and more with her chores. Bobby Dean, the youngest, willingly helped as well. Grandma bought two horses for us to ride. She tried to make our lives sweet and help us move on and not focus on the fact that our mother had abandoned us.

Freda May and I played hard, but we fought just about every day. Since she was the oldest, she would order Anna Kate and me around. Looking back, I can see that it was her way of mothering us. Maybe she expected us to thank her for what she was doing, but we didn't. We resented it. I was extremely strong (still am), so I could beat up my sisters and brother at the same time if arguments got too heated. One time, I swung around to hit Freda May and accidentally struck Grandma on the nose. Her hands quickly covered her face, and she set down with a thud. Suddenly everyone was crying. I thought I must have hit all of them at once. No one had the strength to stop the beatings I gave. One time when Freda May said something I didn't like, I swung around and drove my fist into her face. That angry poke gave her a black eye. The next day at school, she told everyone that I, her sister, had given her a black eye. I was totally humiliated.

"No, Mary Jo wouldn't do that," some objected. But when they asked me about it, I had no answer. Then they knew it was true. After that time, I never hit Freda May again. I had finally learned that violence is not the answer to resolving conflict. Grandma had many words of wisdom to help us deal with our mother's desertion. Gradually, over time, we grew to be independent and became hard-working members of the family. Those good years with Grandma shaped us and gave us a strong foundation for the years ahead. We lost contact with everyone from my mother's side of the family for years with the exception of Grandma Patterson, who would faithfully send birthday cards—always with a dollar enclosed.

Our Family Keeps Expanding

Uncle Hank Ray announced one day that he had found a wife. Unfortunately, she was not a debutante. This woman had been released from a state mental institution but seemed somewhat stable. They were married in 1961 and moved into a house across the road from Grandma.

That winter, snow fell often on the prairie. Drifts piled so high that they didn't melt off until late spring. In the middle of winter, Uncle Hank Ray and his bride installed a wood-burning potbelly stove in the center of their dining room. For some unknown reason, that stove blew up late one night, showering sparks everywhere. Most of them kept burning, and soon the entire house was on fire. Hank Ray and his wife ran out of the house in their nightshirts and bare feet, fleeing the inferno that was engulfing their house. Time after time, Uncle Hank Ray charged into his house, desperately struggling to put out the fire, but without success. Their feet became frostbitten and had to be wrapped, but the fire burned all night long. It was an awful sight.

There was nothing left of their house, so the bride and groom moved into Grandma Brown's house. For many months she soaked and medicated Uncle Hank Ray's feet.

That spring, Uncle Hank Ray and his bride had a baby. The poor woman, mentally unstable, could not handle the responsibilities of marriage and a baby, so men in white coats took her back to the institution, defeated and disoriented. Uncle Hank Ray's baby went to the other grandmother who lived with a sister of his wife. Our uncle remained unmarried and lived with Grandma Brown from that day on for the rest of his life.

The sorrow of losing his wife put Uncle Hank Ray into a tailspin. He began drinking heavily and acting violent and irrational. He belched loudly at the table, ate like a pig, slopped food on the tablecloth, and smelled bad from not bathing. We tried to ignore his eating habits, but sometimes we'd lose our appetite just listening to him eat. He was smart and well educated but would not go to work (or try to find a job). Why wouldn't he go to work? He had a teaching degree, but the only work he ever did was to take care of his pigs, and he did not do much caring for them. Many of them died. Each year, he sold a piece of his five hundred acres of land given to him by Grandma and Grandpa in order to have money to live on. We never understood why he didn't try to accomplish more with his life.

Grandma (Always) Knew Best

Grandma kept one step ahead of us, challenging our creative talents and keeping us occupied with both work and recreation. When we would extract a hard klunger from the coal chute left burning, she would store it until it cooled and then give it to us to paint.

I loved shoveling coal. It made me strong. In a little storage room next to the basement coal shoot, there was a tiny storage room. Freda May made this room into her playhouse. It offered two shelves that were big enough to sleep in. She displayed her dolls and toys in that playhouse, including a set of miniature china dishes with red roses. Every single day, Freda May played with her teacups in her basement playhouse.

A huge oak tree stood in Grandma Brown's backyard. She hired someone to tie a rope to it so we could have some fun. An old tire was tied to the end of the rope. We would swing on that tire for hours on end. I could soar especially high on it by pulling those ropes.

"Be careful," Grandma would warn. "It might break."

"It won't break," I informed Grandma, and it never did.

High up in the air on that swinging tire I felt euphoric, free from the insecurities my parents had created. One of my thoughts came from a conviction that we must have made some big mistakes to cause our mother to leave without even talking to us.

Grandma never became too bothered by the fighting that went on between me and Freda May. She knew we were both strong-willed and would inevitably clash periodically. Grandma focused on teaching us how to be a family again. Grandma taught us to grow a garden, how to be the best seamstresses around, and to become good at taking care of a home. By her example we learned how to love one another and to ignore one another's faults. The years I spent with Grandma were some of the best years for us, and I thank Jesus for each and every one.

Father Takes a Wife

During the last two years of living with Grandma Brown, our dad decided it was time to find a mother for us and a wife for him. His main criterion was to find a woman who did not smoke or drink, so he joined what was called a lonely hearts club. On breaks from his farming he began to travel everywhere looking for a wife. He traveled all through Kansas, drove into Oklahoma, followed up on letters from Missouri, and ran down every lead. We would see Dad occasionally, but our lives were entirely focused on Grandma Brown. We were unprepared for the wife our father found after two years of searching.

Zelda Puddingstone was thirty-five years old and was living with her mother and father in a small Oklahoma town. One eye was straight, and one eye was turned in toward her nose. She did not have an attractive face, and she had unkempt, crooked teeth. Zelda stood all of four feet five inches tall and had a huge stomach.

At every opportunity, Dad slipped off to Oklahoma to see Zelda while Grandma kept running a tight ship at home. All of us were doing well in school, thriving under Grandma Brown's tender loving care—totally unconcerned about our father's plunge into his next monumental change. We helped to bale hay and faithfully did our daily chores.

Bobby Dean was the only child taught to drive the tractor because he was a boy. He spent less and less time with his sisters. When he got home from school, Dad would call him and he would work in the fields until ten o'clock, sometimes even eleven. I was actually stronger than my brother, even though he got to do "man's work." I could lift sixty-pound bales of hay by the time I was eleven years old, but because I was a girl, Dad would not allow me the same treatment he gave my brother.

Grandma was always helping us. She would quietly take Freda

May out on her property and let her practice driving. My sister quickly became an expert driver, and when she got her driver's license, this would soon cause the separation of the family.

Freda May was still doing a great job taking care of the noisy, rutting, lazy pigs.

Our after-school daily chores included slopping the hogs, tending the chicks, milking the cows, straining the milk, and keeping everything neat. Since Freda May and I can't smell, we helped shovel the cow manure into the garden and compost pile. Grandma gave Freda May and me a calf in 1963 as a reward for doing such a good job at the chores. Freda May's calf soon became sick and died. My calf flourished and became very special to me. I put a rope on her and led her around the pasture. She fought me every inch of the way at first, locking her legs and lowering her body, but she was no match for my strength. Freda May told Grandma that I would never get my calf to lead because the calf was so stubborn. Grandma laughed and shook her head. "Mary Jo will get the calf to lead," she replied, "because she is even more stubborn."

Day after day I would lead her around the pasture and Grandma would laugh. After a month Freda May told Grandma, "See, that calf is still not leading." Grandma laughed and said, "We'll see who is the most stubborn." After two months or so, the calf started to lead.

I was in love with that calf. I would brush her every day and feed her long grass outside the fence. After another month the calf followed me everywhere without any rope. I walked my calf to town every Saturday, talking to the townsfolk wanting manure for their garden and visiting. I told them my calf was the most beautiful lady I had ever met. I called her Mother Cow since I did not have a mother. I would take her for walks every day and talk to her as if she were my best friend in life. It was the best gift Grandma could have given me. I still cherish her to this day.

Born Again

No words can ever describe how special Grandma Brown was to us. She taught us moral values, right from wrong, and took us to church regularly even though I did not understand the message about Jesus. At that point, I felt that everybody was solely responsible for his or her own destiny. If bad things happened to you, well, it must be because you needed to pay for your mistakes, right?

Anna Kate accepted Jesus as her Savior during this time with Grandma. Freda May and I did not yet believe. Anna Kate would talk to me about conversion every once in a while.

"I don't know what this Jesus mumbo jumbo is all about. I do know that I don't need any God telling me what to do," I told her.

Anna Kate said, "Jesus is the only way to eternal life."

"That is a mighty narrow road," I told her. "Only one way, huh? Well, let me tell you something. I bet there are a whole heck of a lot of people who don't like hearing that. I don't like it either. I like having many choices." I told her I would believe in a God when our mother walked through that door. I looked hard at Anna Kate. "You know as well as I do that Mom isn't going to walk through that door."

"Why do you say that?" Anna Kate asked.

I said, "She's not going to walk through that door because she doesn't care anything about us. Not even one little bit!"

Anna Kate asked, "How does that make you feel, Mary Jo?"

"Empty," I replied. "Empty as all get out ... and angry."

Anna Kate looked at the pain in my face and said, "You know, Jesus could help you get rid of that pain."

"When my mother walks through that door and not a minute before!" I fired back.

Anna Kate continued to try to persuade me to think about Jesus, but I would always quickly counter with: "The subject is closed until Mom walks through that door."

Anna Kate would shrug and mumble something about my stubbornness. I know she was praying for me. And Grandma kept taking us to church to learn about Jesus. Surely God could not love us as much as He loves other children who have good parents, I reasoned, so I continued to stubbornly reject him. I held on to my rebellious attitude. From 1960 to 1969, we never saw our mother, and we had no idea where she lived. Why wasn't she missing us even a little bit?

Chapter 3

STEPMOTHER RULES

God is our refuge and strength, a very present help in trouble. Therefore will not we fear, though the earth give way, and the mountains fall into the heart of the sea; though its waters roar and foam, and the mountains quake with their surging. Selah.

— Psalm 46:1–3 (NIV)

1964–1967

In 1963, Dad popped the question to Zelda Puddingstone and she accepted. He brought her to Kansas to be married in a church near our farm. We kids attended the quick, simple ceremony and watched them drive off for a honeymoon of several weeks. When Dad returned, he came to see us at Grandma's house and dropped a bombshell. "I want you all to come and live with Zelda and me," he said.

Nobody moved. It was obvious to Dad that none of us wanted to leave Grandma's house, our home, and we all said so. Dad was shocked. He continued to talk to his mother, pushing for us to live with him and Zelda. Each time Grandma refused, saying the children were happy with her and ought not to be moved.

Dad wouldn't give up, so finally Grandma gave in. I'm sure she reasoned that, after all, we were his children. As she helped us pack she promised to come over and see us every day. With Grandma so close, we decided that it would probably be okay.

Building Memories

At first, life with Dad and Zelda wasn't too bad. We noticed that Dad remained tightfisted. He would not pay for any clothes or school activities, so we were forced to ask Grandma Brown to help meet our basic needs. She paid for our clothing, school activity fees, and piano lessons.

We noticed a curious trend: each time Grandma would buy us new clothes, Zelda looked jealous and would go out and buy clothes for herself. Freda May was the first one to notice that when others were not around, Zelda would look for an excuse to antagonize her and accuse my sister of being like our mother.

"Your mother is a prostitute," Zelda would say through clenched teeth, "and you're going to turn out to be just like her. You're stupid and will never amount to anything."

Yelling and screaming soon became part of our family after Zelda came to live with us. She armed herself with a two-by-four board sawed off to approximately two feet to give her power. In addition, her arsenal included kitchen utensils. At first, Zelda made her threats and brandished her weapons only in the presence of Freda May. But Anna Kate and I became more and more uncomfortable in the presence of this woman. We stayed upstairs for as long as we could to avoid any confrontation with her.

Up a narrow, steep staircase with no railings, we climbed to our rooms. It was another world away from Zelda. There we fashioned a house for our paper dolls from a large cardboard box. We played with our dolls for hours at a time, cutting out pictures in old catalogs of everything we needed to furnish our playhouse. We made paper money and actually bought and sold our wares to each other, making profits and taking losses. What fun! We played in the snow during winter months (from November to April) and frolicked in the grass during the summer season.

Dad ruled with a short temper. He had the final say about what television programs we could watch. We did the laundry, cooked most of the meals, cleaned the house, and ran the errands. If we did something our dad didn't like, he would curl his tongue and get ready to punch us. You didn't run and hide. That made matters worse. To this day we're not sure why most of those beatings occurred. Anna Kate has wiped them from her memory.

Life with Dad's Okie

Zelda didn't seem to like any of us children and only focused her attention on Dad. She tolerated us while we cooked and did the laundry, but otherwise we had little association with her. Anna Kate suffered the most. She grew nervous and uncomfortable when violence flared, and it did so quite regularly. Zelda was very jealous of Anna Kate's beauty. Zelda called Anna Kate her favorite prostitute name and a "no good piece of garbage just like her mother." Zelda constantly called us a Whore like our mother. How do I say this the best way?

Zelda had never learned to drive. Now at thirty-five years of age, as Mrs. Loy Brown, she decided she should have the liberating privilege of mastering the automobile. She was too short to see well over the steering wheel and too stiff-necked to turn her head and look behind her when she put the car into reverse, so she relied totally on the rearview mirror. That meant that she continually dented fenders, knocked off chrome strips, and dinged the grill. This irritated Dad, but he said little. Freda May, on the contrary, handled the car like a professional. She never had an accident. In 1964, she got her learner's permit and soon was driving everywhere. She was chauffer for Grandma—to music lessons, grocery store, church, shopping, and any other trip Grandma Brown planned. Zelda did a slow burn every time Freda May's driving was mentioned. This blossomed into downright jealousy. The more Freda May drove, the

Harvesting Hope

more Zelda criticized her. For that reason, my sister began spending more and more time at Grandma's house.

Zelda was also a terrible cook. She burned nearly everything she prepared. She could prepare hamburgers, so they became our staple entrée. They were always cooked too long, so they were a little tough but edible. At times like these we had long, long thoughts about our mother. It didn't help when Zelda would angrily criticize our mother. "She up and gave you away," she reminded us. "What kind of a woman would do that? She's nothing but no good."

We tried to ignore Zelda's growing jealousy and sneaked off to Grandma's house as often as we could. But we absolutely had to attend Dad's church and were never permitted to go to Grandma's church.

The happy day came when Freda May passed her driver's test. This liberated us, but it made Zelda more jealous than ever. One night, a neighbor phoned to confront Zelda about banging into her car. Soon both parties were yelling into the phone with Zelda calling her "a driving maniac" and "a crazy female dog name."

Zelda, called us a Whotre and a Bitch just about every day; What is the best way to relay the message without cussing/When Zelda finally banged down the phone she went looking for Dad. He was nowhere in sight across the fields, so she entered the laundry room where Freda May was working and started putting her down.

"You don't do you share of work around here, young lady," she said.

"I do more than my share of work," Freda May shot back. "If anyone is lazy around here, it's you."

Zelda grabbed her two-by-four board and started after my sister. Freda May ran out of the house with Zelda hard on her trail. I was hanging up clothes as Freda May streaked by yelling, "Zelda is trying to kill me."

Suddenly my sister tripped on a tree root and fell. Zelda bore down on her with her weapon, appearing ready to smash her into the ground. Scared to death, I ran as hard as I could toward my sister. I did a running tackle jump just as Zelda got to Freda May. My weight came down on Zelda and knocked her out cold. I said to

Freda May, "I knocked her plumb out! Maybe she won't remember." Zelda moved a little.

"Run!" I yelled to Freda May, but I didn't have to tell her anything. She streaked for the house, tore through the screen door, and ran up to our bedrooms. I finished hanging up the clothes like nothing had happened. Zelda called for me when she woke up. I went over to her and helped her up. Zelda wanted to know what had happened. I said, "I was hanging up clothes, so I don't know for sure except maybe you tripped on this tree root." I met Freda May upstairs a little later. We hugged. My sister thanked me, and I told her, "Well, I owed you one."

Where would all this fighting lead to? If Zelda had connected with that deadly board, Freda May could have been paralyzed for life or worse. We talked to Grandma Brown, and she spoke with Zelda, but to no avail. "These girls have vivid imaginations," Zelda would always say, brushing off any criticism. But she kept picking fights with Freda May. I chalked it up to jealousy of my sister's expert driving skills. Zelda chased Freda May into the fields of tall corn and Freda May waited there until she thought our interloper had calmed down a bit. Thanks to Freda May, we took Grandma's car to church regularly. Who was this Jesus the pastor at church spoke of so lovingly? I just couldn't buy the fact that God loved us. After all, look at our broken home. If He allowed our mother to leave us without even saying good-bye, what kind of treatment is that for young children? Was there something wrong with us?

Angels Unaware

Hate and Jealousy grew hotter and hotter in the Brown household. While Freda May drove expertly without an accident, Zelda kept sideswiping cars, bending bumpers, and leaving a trail of angry neighbors.

One day, a neighbor's car came around a corner near our house and slowed down. Zelda rear-ended her with a mighty smack. The lady who was driving her car got out and surveyed the damage. She decided that Zelda should pay for fixing her car. As usual, Zelda refused, got into her car, and drove off. The neighbor wasn't going to let the matter drop. She called repeatedly, finally laying down the ultimatum that either Zelda paid to have the car fixed or she would sue. The neighbor called every day and called just before Freda May was to take us to vacation Bible school. A huge, long fight resulted in Zelda hanging up on her in a rage.

Vacation Bible School

In June 1967, vacation Bible school had started in our church. Freda May had asked both Zelda and Grandma for permission to drive us girls to church to enjoy the meetings for kids. Both agreed. Freda May could talk of little else, so eager was she to drive us to church.

That all changed the day the neighbor whom Zelda hit phoned just before we were going to church and got into a heated argument. Zelda slammed down the receiver and swore. Now Zelda was in a rage. Grandma Brown was due at any moment, so we quickly dressed in our good clothes and went downstairs to wait for her. Zelda looked at us for a moment. "Freda May," she said, "you are not a safe driver, and you are not taking any car to vacation Bible school.

"What do you mean?" Freda May replied. "I've never hit anybody. Never even came close to hitting anyone."

"Well, you are not driving anywhere today. Just get that straight right now."

Freda May was devastated. She looked at Zelda's evil grin and said, "You are the unsafe driver in this family. You keep hitting everybody."

Zelda's eyes popped open wide. She was beyond furious! She started to scream at the top of her lungs at my sister.

"What's your problem?" Freda May asked several times. Freda May turned to look out the door happy to see that Grandma's car was just coming into view. Zelda ran into her bedroom while Anna Kate went outside to wait for Grandma coming down the lane, and

I saw Freda May move to the doorway facing outside looking for Grandma. I decided to look back hearing a noise when suddenly Zelda came rushing out of her bedroom with her two-by-four. Freda May's back was toward Zelda. Anna Kate was in the yard watching Grandma pull up. I tried to stop the two-by-four just before Zelda smashed it against Freda May's back so hard that she went flying out of the house and down the porch, landing in a heap six feet from the door. Freda May was knocked unconscious. Surely Freda May's back was broken.

I started to run out to help Freda May, but Zelda stopped me. "Are you crazy?" I yelled at her. "You could have killed her."

"You will never see her again," Zelda hissed, gritting her teeth. "Freda May is not allowed ever again to enter this house."

I said, "You don't have the power to do that!"

Zelda said, "Watch me."

Grandma saw Freda May on the ground. She ran to Freda May just as Anna Kate and I started fighting with Zelda. "Go back to Oklahoma," I cried. "You're not our mother."

Zelda was determined never to let Freda May into her house again. Grandma talked to Zelda for a long time, but to no avail. Finally, Grandma helped Freda May into her car and took her home. She told me and Anna Kate that she would call later. Zelda smiled an evil smile and ordered us to get back into the house. Anna Kate and I were too angry to speak. How could Zelda be so evil? My hatred of the intruder ran deep. Why did this woman have so much power? How could she be allowed to separate sisters?

A few hours later Dad came in from the fields. Zelda told him her version of what had happened, but Dad said nothing. I couldn't believe it. I ran over to him and cried, "Dad, she's a liar! Freda May did nothing wrong! Zelda is just jealous of Freda May's being such a good driver." Still Dad said nothing. "Let Anna Kate and I go with Grandma and Freda May. Please?" Dad remained silent. He seemed to be struggling with an inner rage.

Now completely engulfed in anger, I cried, "Are you going to allow that female dog to split us up? I hate you for this."

Dad stood up and hit me so hard I flew across the room and landed on the wall. Anna Kate thought I was dead. Anna Kate ran to my side and pulled on my arms, struggling to help me up. The wall was indented from my body. We hobbled up the stairs to our rooms, sick, disappointed, angry, and afraid—sobbing as if our hearts would break.

As she promised to do, Grandma phoned every day to see how we were doing and to report on Freda May. I was amazed to hear, "Freda May's back is fine." Then Grandma asked for Zelda. She pleaded with the woman to let Freda May return home. Zelda smiled her evil smile and dug in her heels. "There's no way," she said. She said it with a smile—the kind of sinister joy an angry person gets when she has her own way.

Grandma prayed and prayed. She had never been able to challenge her sons to live better lives. Anna Kate and I felt so tortured that we made plans to run away and we told Grandma we might. Having our sister torn from us and not being able to see her was pure agony.

"Until you are fifteen," Grandma told me on the phone, "Kansas law says you cannot choose where you live." Dad and Zelda could force Anna Kate to remain with them, but Freda May and I were ready to split. I asked Anna Kate what she would do if we left and Dad forced her to come back without me. She said she would kill herself. We would have to wait to leave until Anna Kate was fifteen. It was the only way to protect her and keep from being separated. Wasn't there anybody that could help us? Grandma Brown kept praying for an answer.

Being ripped from her sisters put Freda May into a kind of depression. Grandma would call almost every day to see how Anna Kate and I were doing. Zelda was fairly good to us during this period. She was so happy to see the effect the separation had on us sisters. To my knowledge, Grandma only confronted Dad with the situation a few times. Dad would not answer Grandma Brown either. Finally in August 1967 Grandma decided to take Freda May away from Kansas and end the torture of Freda May not seeing us. Grandma called for me and told me she was taking Freda May to Oklahoma and putting her in school down there.

"Can Anna Kate and I go, too?" I pled with Grandma. Grandma talked to Dad and Zelda one last time and both said we had to remain with them. We knew the risk of running, and we couldn't take the chance. We cried ourselves to sleep every night and found our contempt of Zelda growing. I realized after Freda May had left how very much I had depended on her to ease the pain of our mother's leaving. I had not always been kind to her. She mothered me and Anna Kate to ease the pain of our mother's leaving, but I thought she was being bossy. Now that my sister was going away, I realized how childish my actions and attitudes had been and how much I'd miss her. I think God gave me the wisdom to understand what a help my sister had been over the years.

I phoned Grandma and asked to talk to my sister and tell her how much I loved her. Just as Freda May was coming to the phone, Zelda grabbed the receiver out of my hand. "You will never talk to Freda May again," she growled. I was so enraged I felt like killing her right on the spot. Zelda told Freda May not to phone. "You will never talk to Mary Jo again," she said. "And you will never see her again." Then Zelda slammed down the receiver, turned to me, and smiled. I turned and signaled Anna Kate. We both ran upstairs where we cried our hearts out.

Kneeling at the Cross

Grandma called Zelda the next day and told her that she was coming to visit before she left for Oklahoma. Once she was at our house, Grandma took Anna Kate and me for a walk. I asked, "Do you think that if we ran they would find us?"

Grandma said, "They would find us sooner or later."

Anna Kate quickly said, "I'll kill myself if they bring me back here by myself! I will!"

I said, "Now, there's no need for that kind of talk. I'll stay with you."

"I'm leaving tomorrow," Grandma said, "because Freda May is being tortured so badly. I hate the idea of leaving both of you. I've tried to talk to your father and Zelda, but it doesn't do any good."

Grandma was visibly upset as she spoke. Suddenly she turned to Anna Kate and asked, "Have you received Jesus as your savior?"

Anna Kate nodded. "Yes, I have. You know that, Grandma. We've talked about it many times."

Grandma just smiled. Then she turned to me. "Mary Jo, have you accepted Jesus as your Savior?"

"No," I shot back. "I have not. He let my mother leave me, and now you're leaving me, too. Grandma, I never thought I'd see the day you would leave me! Jesus doesn't love me, or all these bad things would not be happening to me! Other kids have parents who love them. They don't have all these terrible things happening to them. I know He's there, but I won't accept Him."

Tears ran down Grandma's cheeks as she hugged me. Then she turned to my sister. "Anna Kate, this is going to take a while."

"Okay, I'll be playing on the swings," said Anna Kate. "It might take all day. I know how stubborn Mary Jo is."

As Anna Kate ran off to the playground, Grandma and I sat down on the porch. She turned to me and said, "Mary Jo, I never thought it would come when I would have to leave you. Your mother made a choice, and it has affected us all. She did not try to keep you. Instead, she left your father for another man. Jesus always gives us choices to do good or bad in this world. There might be many reasons why your mother chose to leave all of you, but nevertheless, it has affected us all. Some mistakes in life are irrevocable and hurt others terribly. I am sure that before her life is over, your mother will be very sorry she left everyone.

"Mary Jo, do you think no other children have suffered from a parent's leaving?" Grandma asked.

"No," I said. "I know others have gone through that pain as well."

Grandma lowered her eyes and folded her hands. "Mary Jo," she continued, "you and Anna Kate are very special to me. Not everyone would be as strong going through your pain. Both of you are precious to Jesus. I'm sure Jesus has shed tears over your mother's decision, but He had to let her make the decision, no matter how much it hurt everyone else." Grandma sighed and continued, "I have wondered for months what to do with this ugly situation. I've been praying night and day. I never dreamed Zelda would become so ugly. But Mary Jo, I can't leave you without knowing that you have Jesus."

"Why is that so important, Grandma?" I asked.

"Mary Jo, you need His strength to get through this hateful situation without hating others. You won't make it without Jesus. Jesus is our protector. We can take refuge in Him and learn to forgive others through Him as He has forgiven your sins."

I said, "Sometimes I feel all this hate for my dad and Zelda because of all the bad things they've done. And they just keep on doing it! When will they pay for it? It's hard not to hate them."

"God gives us strength to overcome hate," Grandma explained. "Judgment day comes when we die or when Jesus comes for us. We are accountable for the good and bad we do on earth. You can be sure that Jesus will have a word or two to say to Zelda about what she did on earth. But Jesus protects and directs His own children. Mary Jo, will you accept Jesus now? You need Him more than ever. He will never leave you. He loved you enough to die for you."

"Grandma, you do know that we're goners, don't you? There is no hope for us. One hit with that two-by-four and we are dead. We are going to have to take those hits for years! Zelda is evil and very powerful! Too powerful for us to survive the beatings." I hesitated. Several minutes went by. Finally I said, "Grandma, it's not going to make any difference."

She came close to me and spoke softly, "Mary Jo, this is the most important decision you will ever make. Jesus is powerful! He has the power to get you through this. He will be your refuge. All things are possible with Jesus!"

"Just how sure are you about this Jesus of yours?" I asked.

"Jesus is the Son of the almighty God of this world. He is God!" Grandma replied. "I am as sure of this as I am that I'm standing here right now. If you don't accept Jesus, you won't make it, and if you don't make it, neither will Anna Kate."

I looked over at Anna Kate, and she looked so scared and fragile. I decided I could not protect her. I needed help!

I hesitated. "All right, Grandma, I'll accept Him right now. Show me the way." Grandma was shocked with her mouth open. Grandma said, "Mary Jo, are you sure?"

I said, "I am accepting Him with everything that I am."

My dear sweet grandmother prayed for me as I gave my heart to the Lord forever. Grandma called Anna Kate back and spoke softly to both of us. "I don't know how bad things are going to get," she said. "If they get really bad, call and I will come back to Kansas to help. Whatever happens, cry out to Jesus for protection. He will give you the strength you need to get through it."

Then Grandma read 1 Corinthians 10:13 (NIV): "No temptation has seized you except what is common to man. And God is faithful; he will not let you be tempted beyond what you can bear. But when you are tempted, he will also provide a way out so that you stand up under it."

"You two know that I love you just as much as I love Freda May, don't you? Grandma asked.

We both nodded and answered yes.

"Then trust Jesus as the only true living God and pray for strength and wisdom. He will make you strong."

"Will Jesus be coming for us someday?" I asked.

"You can count on it," Grandma promised. "Start reading your Bibles every day so you can be closer to God. He is stronger than anyone or anything on this earth. He will make you strong."

"Grandma," I asked, "do you think Jesus will come back before you die?"

My dear little Granny smiled again. "It doesn't matter. Either way I get to be with Him, and that's what I'm looking forward to." She hugged us both. "Jesus won't leave you as I am," she added. "He will always be with you. You two must be very special to God because most people would not be strong enough to get through this hateful situation. I don't want to leave you, but I don't know what else to do."

Grandma got into her car and rolled down her window. "I love you!" she called. Her car went down the road and was gone. I kept staring at the road so grieved at losing Grandma. Finally Anna Kate said, "Jo, are you all right?"

I said "Heck no! I just had my heart ripped in two parts. Zelda never should have had the power to separate us!" I hesitated, and then I said, "And I just accepted this Jesus, and I can't even see Him with my own two eyes!" I swung my arms wide and said, "You can bet your life that I am checking Him out. I am not like some folks; I am either all in or I'm out."

We never saw her or had a call from Grandma for the next three years. Anna Kate and I wondered if Zelda had threatened to hurt us if she called.

That night Anna Kate and I prayed together for the first time. We prayed for strength and wisdom as Grandma Brown had told us to do. We prayed that God would bring us all together again. I thanked God for Anna Kate, Bobby Dean, and Mother Cow, because I still had them.

Chapter 4

THE DARKEST YEARS

He delivered me from my strong enemy, from those who hated me: for they were too strong for me.

—Psalm 18:17 (NKJV)

Late 1960s

I started reading the Bible every spare moment I could. Anna Kate would say, "You sure are reading a lot."

I'd say, "Still checking."

At church the Sunday after Grandma and Freda May left, we found a pamphlet published by a Christian organization. It stated that if we memorized Bible verses every day we could get a free week of camp. With the zeal of desperados we began memorizing the Bible verses like clockwork. It soon paid off. That summer in 1968, we climbed on a bus with other kids and rode to Salina, Kansas. Everything was free, including the bus fare to summer camp. It was a loving, nurturing, and nonviolent atmosphere. It was so enjoyable that we hated to return home to Dad and Zelda. But all good things on earth come to an end, and soon we were rumbling back home with dread in our hearts.

As we expected, the floors at home were dusty and dirty. The kitchen table was filthy with a buildup of food and dirt. Dad's sloppy eating habits, like those of Uncle Hank Ray, sickened our stomachs. Our uncle would eat food dropped on the floor and laugh that it flavored the food.

Dad continually told us that he and all of us were stupid, not like other people. He rambled on about killing presidents because of this or that. His own lack of farming techniques, his inability to maintain his equipment well, and his poor planting schedules and decisions on selling his crops meant he had to borrow money on the land just to be able to make a living.

Anna Kate and I were getting used to our new routine. I did the ironing, the garden work, and kept the lawn cared for. Anna Kate did the dishes and trash. We both cleaned the house. After a week or so I was telling Anna Kate how much it bothered me that I could not apologize to Freda May when we heard a whining saw noise.

Anna Kate said, "What's that?"

I said, "I don't know, let's check it out." We went downstairs into the backyard to the corner of the house to peek toward that noise. We could see Zelda sawing up ten-foot two-by-four boards into two-foot lengths.

Anna Kate said, "Zelda is going to try to kill us with those two-by-fours!"

I said, "Jesus is the powerful almighty God, and we need to be still and know that He is God! Psalm 46:10."

Anna Kate's mouth flew open in shock. After a few minutes, I said, "You can close your mouth anytime now."

Anna Kate replied, "I didn't think you would ever get it!"

I replied, "Some of us take a little bit longer than others."

Anna Kate said, "Well, if you ask me, it's in the nick of time."

I took another look and said, "Can't argue with that; busy little bee, isn't she?" I asked Anna Kate if she wouldn't mind going upstairs because I wanted to check something out in my garden and would only be a few minutes. I went to the garden and got on my knees. I prayed to the almighty God, "Jesus, we are in a heap of trouble down here. I have been wondering about You. You are the only one who can save us. If it is all right with You, let me take the hits from the two-by-fours. Will You protect my sister? She is scared out of her mind of being beat up or killed. If You really love us, will You shield us from the top of our heads to the bottom of our feet? You are our only hope. We cannot make it without You. Zelda is too strong for us. I pray that You will give us the strength and wisdom to endure. Give us Your peace and comfort that only You can give. We only have days before two-by-fours come our way. You know which day it's going to be. Help us to totally trust in You and not be afraid. Thank You, Jesus! Amen."

Three weeks after Grandma and Freda May left, Anna Kate and I started school. We asked Dad for lunch money, and he told us that he would give it to us if we promised not to write or call or contact Grandma Brown in any way. We had no choice but to say yes to him, so we promised that we wouldn't contact her.

Okie Summers to Remember

The only thing Anna Kate was thankful for about Zelda was that she came from Oklahoma. The reason was that my sister was able to go there on vacation to visit Zelda's family and had the best times of her life. Zelda's brother, Brad, and his wife treated her like royalty. They had a son and a daughter who were fun to be with. That first summer I was also invited. What fun we had together.

Settling Scores

But September always came, and we cried when it was time to return to Kansas and head back to school. One reason we cried was that our dad would not buy us new clothing. He wouldn't even give us money for necessities like underwear. Even though we would work hard at school to learn, kids made fun of us because our clothes were too tight and worn thin.

One pretty girl, Erica, made fun of my dress once too often. In retaliation, I yanked on her pretty dress in a burst of anger. "How pretty is your dress now?" I asked.

Everyone was shocked and couldn't figure out how I had the strength to make a six-inch tear in that dress and ran to tell the teacher. She requested that I stay after class.

"Did you rip the dress, Mary Jo?" the teacher asked sweetly.

"Yes," I said. "I was tired of being made fun of all the time."

The teacher carefully looked me over. "Why don't you have many clothes? I notice that you wear the same ones every week."

"Well," I replied, "my dad won't buy us any clothes. But I plan to work next summer and get some money for clothes."

The teacher looked at the floor. "Mary Jo, I know you are in a tough situation at home," she said, "but you cannot ever harm someone else's clothes. I will talk to Erica about making fun of you. Will you promise not to do this again?"

Nodding, I gave her my word that I wouldn't do it again. She asked me to wait until tomorrow to apologize.

The next day when I apologized to Erica, she cried. "You have ruined my dress forever," she wailed. "My mom can't fix it, and it was my favorite!"

I was shocked. Grandma Brown had shown us how to mend practically anything. "I can fix it, if you will trust me," I promised.

Erica hesitated. "All right," she said. "I'll bring it tomorrow." The bodice had not torn, just the gathered skirt stitching to the bodice. I was lucky. "I'll have this as good as new tomorrow," I told her.

That night, I had the dress done in ten minutes. I felt good. And I felt even better the next day when Erica thanked me and gave me a big hug. Some mistakes you make in life you can't fix, but this one I could fix. What's more, Erica never made fun of me again. That wasn't true of everybody. A boy name Jeff came toward her on the playground one day with a scowl on his face. Erica screamed. "You've made fun of me once too often," he said. I didn't see any teacher on that side of the playground.

"What's going on?" I asked him.

"I'm going to make her pay," he snarled.

"Jeff," I said, my hands on my hips, "you're not going to touch her. You have no right to hit her."

He stopped and looked at me. "Why are you defending her? She's done nothing around here but act better than everyone else. She keeps making fun of us°..."

Jeff raised his arm as if to hit Erica, but I caught it in midair. I entwined my fingers with his. Jeff couldn't believe how strong I was. I tweaked his hand against his body so hard that he hollered. "Don't underestimate my strength," I told him. "Others have and they've paid a price. You have no right making Erica pay for her mistakes when you haven't paid for yours."

"I don't know what you're talking about," Jeff said.

"Well, what about you cheating on that history test last week? I saw you, and God knows a whole lot more about you. Worry about cleaning up your own backyard before you worry about cleaning up Erica's."

I let go of his hand, and Jeff listened as I pressed on: "I used to beat up my sisters and no one stopped me. Oh, how I wish someone had. Maybe no one had the strength. There are maggots all over my slate, and I'm going to try to do better and be someone God is just a little proud of. Someday you'll thank me for stopping you. Remember, you're not touching her! So get going."

Jeff grudgingly walked off, shaking his head. After he was gone, I looked at Erica. "You know," I said to her, "there was a lot of truth in Jeff's statement about you making fun of others. If you don't quit acting better than others, there's going to be a day you pay for it. I might not be here next time to save you."

Erica looked at me condescendingly. "Oh, you don't know anything!" A few days later, Erica came to school with bruises on her arm, shoulders, and face as well as a black eye. Jeff had caught up with her after school the day before. They had exchanged words, and Jeff had lost his temper. Parents were called to the school several times for conferences with the principal and some teachers. The next day I saw Erica on the playground, embarrassed by her bruises. "Are you okay?" I asked.

"Yes," she said. "You know, Mary Jo, you were right about paying a price."

A tear ran down my cheek. "Actually, I had hoped that I was wrong," I said, giving Erica a big hug and trying to comfort her by talking about other things. I thanked her again for her forgiveness after I ripped her dress, and I made her laugh by saying, "Aren't I the best seamstress around?" Then I went looking for Jeff. I found him on the monkey bars with a couple of his friends.

"Jeff, have you learned a lesson from hitting Erica?" I asked.

He smirked at me. "I taught her a lesson. She won't act better than me anymore."

I leveled my gaze at him. "Since you are now giving out lessons," I said, "learn this one. If you ever harm her again, I will make sure that everyone in this school knows about your mistakes—family, friends, and teachers. I've been trying hard to clean up my backyard, but I can watch your backyard and make sure everyone knows every mistake you make so they can judge you like you judge Erica. No tellin' what my backyard will look like when this is all over with, but I can do it if I have to." I quickly turned toward another schoolmate. "Hey, Brad!" I called. "Did you know that Jeff cheated on his history test by sneaking the answers off the teacher's desk early in the morning and writing them on the palm of his hand?"

Brad frowned. "Jeff, you bragged to us that you studied half the night to get that A on the test."

I shook my finger at Jeff. "You'd better start being perfect. It's easy to make Erica's mistake of acting better than others when you have a lot of money. You and I might make the same mistake, too, if we don't watch out. Let God judge her. If there is one thing I've learned in life it's that I don't have to beat someone up because he or she does something I don't like."

Jeff never hit anyone again, to my knowledge. I hope what I said helped him.

"Someday We'll Have Peace"

Sharon became my best friend at school. One of eight children, she had very little money to spend. As one of my good friends,

Sharon helped me out every chance she had. She would come over to my house regularly and couldn't believe the abuse that went on.

One evening she spent the night with me. I was embarrassed by my panties. They had been darned so many times that the material the darning was attached to was wearing out. You could see right through the material. I told Dad that I could do without any other clothes if I could just have a few changes of underwear.

"No!" he said. He became angry and punched me hard, throwing me across the room. Sharon could not believe her eyes. After that, she helped me sew by hand new material over the worn-out sections to the elastic on both sides, hoping it would last until I could buy new panties.

"We are so poor," Anna Kate murmured, adding, "but someday we will be rich and have twenty pairs of underwear."

She and I split the chores. I did the ironing and washed the clothes; Anna Kate washed and dried the dishes. Other chores we teamed up on. My sister and I kept up our grades all that year, lying low at home to avoid any trouble. After doing the supper dishes, we'd slip upstairs for the evening.

Six months passed without any major trouble, but we noticed Zelda's increasing jealousy toward Anna Kate because of her beauty. "Don't comb your hair," I'd advise my sister. "Look as ugly as you can so Zelda won't envy you." But it didn't work. Zelda picked on Anna Kate anyhow. She called her "an ugly prostitute name like your mother," I mentioned before that she called us a Whore and a bitch every day. How do we say this? and cut her down in many other ways. These threats and insinuations made Anna Kate more and more nervous. By spring of 1968, Zelda's hate and jealousy toward my sister had progressed to the hate stage. Zelda constantly called Anna Kate names, threatening her and trying to strike her in various parts of her body. If I wasn't nearby, Anna Kate would yell for me and run fast to get away from Zelda. We made up a code in case we got separated. We had to think of something Zelda would never say. Anna Kate thought, "Jesus loves you," would never come out of her mouth. Meanwhile, I was growing stronger by the day, lifting hay bales, caring for the animals, and doing other farm work. The time came when I had to physically hold Zelda off. I had to become Anna Kate's shadow, protecting her daily. I would always check to make sure Zelda was far away on the farm before I would leave the house to work in the garden, pick cherries and other fruit off the trees, and hang out laundry to dry. I worked a quarter acre garden that had a peach and cherry tree on each end. I kept the garden so clean from weeds that everyone who saw it would say, "How dare a weed grow there!" and laugh. I tried to be careful if I had too much work to check in with Anna Kate. I never knew when Zelda would drive in and start trouble with Anna Kate.

As Anna Kate was cleaning the kitchen, I told her I would check on the garden and see if a weed had dared to grow. I walked up there and sure enough, many weeds had sprung up. I worked methodically pulling up weeds, hoeing, and then mulching the tomato plants. As I was mulching the last tomato plant, I noticed all the leaves were gone off of two branches. It didn't look like the branches had died. What's going on here? I started inspecting the branches closer and saw a big, green worm-looking creature on the underside of one of the bare branches eating away. "The nerve!" I said. "Eating up my tomato plants." I took the hoe and edged him off the plant to the ground. "You're a goner!" I smashed my hoe into its worm body hard. The worm's guts went flying everywhere. I had worm guts all over me now. I headed back to the house not realizing how much time had gone by. I got close to the house and saw Zelda's truck. I ran like lighting to the house and opened the door. I saw Zelda threatening Anna Kate with the sawed off two-by-four. I said, "Jesus, let me get there in time!" Anna Kate had her arms over her head ducking to the floor to protect herself from the weapon. I reached out my left arm and over Anna Kate just in time as the two-by-four hit my arm. I heard a huge *crack*! I thought my arm would be broken for sure. The two-by-four went sailing in the family room. I pushed Zelda back, telling her to stop, but she was strong enough to hold her ground. We kept pushing each other, but I was not strong enough to push her back. Zelda said, "You are going to the floor! I am taking you down."

The pushing continued, and Zelda was slowly edging me backward because she was stronger. I called out to Jesus to hold me up, and I remained steady. Zelda finally got tired and headed back to the fields. It shook me up that Zelda was stronger than me. Our lives totally depended on Jesus since we had an enemy too strong for us. Anna Kate asked if my arm was hurt. I rubbed my arm where the two-by-four hit and felt nothing. I said no. Anna Kate said, "I want to see that two-by-four. It hit your arm with a noise like a bomb going off." We decided to look for it. The two-by-four was in the next room about twenty feet away under the couch. It had totally splintered and broken like a sledgehammer had hit it. Anna Kate said, "Jesus is saving our butts!"

I was so touched that Jesus had stopped that two-by-four that I said to Anna Kate in tears, "Jesus really does loves us and is watching over us."

Anna Kate said, "This is a miracle. That two-by-four should have taken your arm off. Is your arm sore anywhere?"

I said, "No, not at all," running my right arm over my left looking for a sore, bruised area but finding nothing at all.

The next week at school, I went to Mr. Johnson, the teacher for Future Farmers of America (FFA). I went over to his unused two-by-fours and asked him about the strength of the wood compared to the human bone in case of an accident. Mr. Johnson explained that the two-by-four is approximately twenty times stronger. I asked, "What if your arm hit the two-by-four with force and made it splinter?"

Mr. Johnson said, "That would be a miracle! Your arm should break every time long before the two-by-four. That's why I teach every student to know the risks of farming and the best way to protect yourself from accidents. Trust me, the two-by-four will always win any battle with the human bone. The human bone has no chance."

I said, "Thanks so much for the information. I'll be careful."

I continued to take piano lessons after Grandma had left. I was becoming better at the piano and playing harder pieces all the time. I have a photographic memory and could memorize an amazing amount of pieces. Mrs. Pope enjoyed the recitals that showed off her students' hard work. How was she getting paid? I was afraid to ask and gratefully focused on the beautiful music and not on the ugly fighting that happened every day.

"Just get through this year," I told Anna Kate. "Then you'll be fifteen, and you can choose where you want to live."

We had not heard from Freda May or Grandma for nearly two years now. Zelda told us continually, "Your sister and grandmother don't love you anymore, or they would have called to see how you are doing." We ignored this, figuring that they had tried to call, but Zelda wouldn't let us talk. We never knew the truth. We did know that they loved us, and we were praying for a reunion soon.

In May that year, Anna Kate and I discussed strategies for the work and how to avoid leaving Anna Kate alone if Zelda was anywhere close. Anna Kate asked me, "Will it really ever end?"

"Yes!" I said emphatically. "We will have peaceful lives someday. Jesus has heard our prayers and will let us stand up through this ugly situation. I don't know when it we will be, but this will end."

Months of fighting Zelda to keep her from slugging Anna Kate began to take a toll on me. Zelda was far away on the farm one day, so I climbed a large evergreen tree that was three stories high. I was telling Jesus how I didn't like it down on earth. I asked how there was so much evil down there, and let Jesus have an earful. Then I stopped to listen. It was so peaceful I could have stayed there forever. There was no evil up there, no hatred, and no strife. I began talking to God: "I want to be with You. I hate it down there. It's so nice here. No one can hurt me here. There's no fighting up here." A small breeze came by and cooled my body. I said, "That feels so good!"

Just then I heard screams below. I looked down and saw Zelda chasing Anna Kate. "Mary Jo! Mary Jo!" my sister was screaming. I looked back at the sky as I prepared to descend. "I get it, Jesus. I can make a difference down there, but I can't do diddly squat up here. I will trust You with everything down there, and I will never come back up here again!"

I zoomed down that tree like a rocket, worrying about my sister. On the ground I couldn't find her for a while. Now I was really frightened. Zelda stood in the kitchen with an evil scowl on her face. "I don't know where your sister is," she said. I wondered if she had gotten to my sister while I was up there in the tree. I had to find her.

I hunted desperately, going building to building using the secret code, but I didn't find her until I entered the cow feeding area with the cow stalls. I did not see her, but just before I left I said, "Jesus loves You," and Anna Kate jumped out of the hay more angry than a hornet!

"Where were you?" Anna Kate sobbed when she saw me. "Zelda chased me to beat me up, and I didn't do anything. I screamed and screamed, but you didn't come."

"Anna Kate," I explained calmly, "I was up at the top of the evergreen tree talking to God. It was so peaceful up there. I didn't think about what could happen down here. I was just so sick of the bad going on here that I wanted to get away."

"Mary Jo," my sister sobbed, "I need you down here. I can't fight Zelda. I'm not strong enough. She tried to kill me. I barely outran her! It will be worse next time. Promise me you won't go up there again."

I gave her my word and helped her into the house. I got her all cleaned up in the bathroom when we went upstairs. I comforted her until she fell asleep. Then I went downstairs and looked for Zelda. She was in the living room watching TV. When she saw me coming, she smiled a happy, evil smile.

"Zelda," I said, folding my arms across my chest, "the next time you try to hurt Anna Kate, you'll be dealing with me. Do you get it? You're going to have to fight me to get to Anna Kate."

Zelda said nothing. She really did not look worried.

Springtime Calves

Mother Cow had three calves over the last three years and was pregnant with her fourth calf. It was time to give birth to her calf, but this time was different. As much as Mother Cow tried, she could not make any progress. My dad thought the calf was turned around. Dad tried and tried but could not get the calf turned around. Dad looked at me and said, "I can't get the calf turned right. Both of them are going to die."

I cried "No! Call the vet! He can get the calf turned around." Dad said "We don't have the enough money to call the vet!" I said, "Let's sell four of the bigger calves, and you will have enough money to call the vet and grocery money for months. Please, Dad, Mother Cow cannot die!"

Dad hesitated, "Does this cow mean that much to you?"

I said, "Yes and a million times more! The herd was thirty-four when Grandma left, now we have fifty-seven. Grandma won't mind, so please!"

Dad hesitated again but finally said, "Okay." The vet came and got the calf turned around and saved Mother Cow and the calf. I was so happy!

Summertime Labors

In May, just a week or two before school got out, Mother Cow and most of the herd usually crossed over a barbed wire fence to get into the cornfield next to it. Those great big leaves on the stalk looked mighty tasty. Many of the cows' teats and other areas were cut badly. Dad decided to tie the legs of the cows that needed milking. Each cow he milked fought him. They jerked around and tried to kick him. I got home late from school that day to see Mother Cow's leg tied up with Dad trying to milk her. Mother Cow's leg got loose and kicked my dad and knocked him off the stool. Dad said to me, "Let her die. She is too stubborn to be milked."

I went up to Mother Cow and talked to her about staying in the pasture from now on. I said lovingly, "Mother Cow, this is going to hurt, but you will die if I don't milk you, and I love you way too much for that! I just love you so much!" I gave her a kiss on the nose. I took the rope off and got the stool. I looked at the cuts on her teats and they were deep. I started milking, and Mother Cow did not move a muscle. Dad could not believe his eyes. He stood there watching until I was almost done then he left. I put salve on all her cuts to help her heal. I hugged her again. Mother Cow had been so good. I said, "Every day will hurt less." She followed me as I did my chores and put salve on the other cows' cuts.

My friend Sharon told me about work in the cornfields detasseling stalks for $1.25 per hour in the summer. It would be enough money to buy clothes for us. I talked to Dad about the opportunity to work for school clothes. He was very agreeable since he had no money for school clothes. I said, "Dad, I am happy to work; I have a ride to Sharon's on Monday mornings and will be back on Friday nights. I need to know that you will take care of the cows Monday to Friday while I'm working in the cornfields. Will you?" Dad said yes.

One weekend morning after it had rained for two days previously, Anna Kate and I walked out of the house to check on the cows. There was this beautiful rainbow that took up almost the whole sky. I said, "I can see Jesus and the work of His hands with my own two eyes! I was blinder than a bat!"

Anna Kate said, with a smile, "Not anymore!"

I was so happy and said, "Yes, not anymore!" Then we high-fived and went to the pasture to check on the cows.

School ended the first week of June. Anna Kate collected our grades (mostly Bs and Cs) and then it was out to the fields to detassel corn for me. The she would be off to Oklahoma to spend the summer with one of Zelda's brothers' families. But Dad and Zelda weren't leaving for two weeks. I couldn't leave Anna Kate alone with Zelda while I worked in the fields, so I spoke to the forelady. "No," she said, "your sister can't come with you." I was desperate. Privately I explained our situation at home. "My sister could set up the lunch table and do any chores needed—for no money," I said. "I promise to work twice as hard as the average worker for no extra pay the entire summer if you would let Anna Kate come with me for two weeks.

"I'll talk it over with my assistant," she said, "and let you know in ten minutes."

Sharon and I waited, hardly breathing. "Okay," she said when she returned, "two weeks only."

I gave her a big hug. "Thank you," I squealed.

Working those cornfields was hard work especially for the short ladies. At five foot three inches I had to stand on my tiptoes to detassel the corn. I was amazed how strong my calves were. I could stay on my tiptoes all day long with ease. This made me five foot six inches and able to detassel the corn with speed like the tall ladies. We started working at 7:00 a.m. Anna Kate kept busy doing errands most of the time. When she had nothing to do, she would follow behind me in the rows. I worked very hard and fast because I had promised the forewoman. I could finish two rows for every one of an average worker, except when I ran into trouble with bumblebees. Every worker got stung. I tried to outrun them, but the bees were always faster and I got stung, too.

One morning, as Anna Kate followed along, we came upon a stalk with bumblebees circling. "Couldn't you just skip this one?" my sister asked.

"No," I replied. "Skipping one tassel could mess up the field for a mile. Go back twenty feet and run."

As I reached up and snipped the tassel, the bees angrily headed for the destroyer. I ran as fast as I could down that row, but I still got stung. Other ladies on the crew enjoyed my sprints.

One day Anna Kate said, "I've been wondering why you work like a maniac. Does your hard work have something to do with my being here?"

I looked at my sister and smiled. "You always were the wise one," I said. "Yes, I promised them I'd work doubly hard if you could be with me. But a little hard work never hurt me. Just think! We will have enough money to buy our own clothes. We can go shopping!"

My sister smiled and said no more. Soon it was time for Anna

Kate to go to Oklahoma. I was happy to see my sister get away and have some fun with others. Anna Kate stayed with Zelda's brother. Amazing enough, it was just blocks from where Freda May and Grandma lived, but Anna Kate never knew it. Zelda ordered her brother never to tell Grandma and Freda May that Anna Kate came to spend the summer.

I stayed with Sharon for the entire summer while we worked in the fields. Each weekend I would go home to check on Mother Cow. She had dried up, so I didn't need to milk her that summer. It was an answer to my prayer. If she hadn't dried up, I couldn't have worked in the cornfields.

Now Mother Cow was pregnant again. I was happy about that because all of her children were college money for me. She had had four calves over four years. This should bring me at least $1,000 toward college tuition, maybe more.

With Anna Kate gone, I would talk to Mother Cow by the hour, telling her my plans to buy clothes and go to college. I even prayed with Mother Cow, vowing never to leave her.

The Bovine Massacre

Dad finished cultivating the corn by the end of June. He decided to bulldoze the ground around the creek and pond that the cows drink out of in the big pasture at the back part of our property. He reshaped the pond and moved it farther from the road. He never told me he was doing the work or moved the cows to the front pasture. He bulldozed on Monday, and it rained several inches on Tuesday and Wednesday. The next afternoon, the cows tried to drink from the pond. They sank deeper and deeper into the muck. Dad never checked on them.

When I got home on Friday, Mother Cow was not there. I asked if she had been up to the house in the last few days.

"No," Dad said.

I knew something was wrong. "Dad, something is really wrong

here. Mother Cow would be here if she could make it. Where are the cows now?"

"In the back pasture," Dad said.

"When did you check on them last?"

"I didn't have time this week. Hop into the truck. We'll check on them now."

I asked, "Did anything happen while I was gone?"

Dad said, "I bulldozed around the creek and pond Monday."

I said, "Dad, it rained Tuesday and Wednesday! The dirt will become muck. You promised to watch the cows to make sure they were okay." I started praying, "Jesus, don't let it be as bad as it could be."

Dad drove me to the back pasture. The scene before us was devastating. I will never forget it. The whole herd of cows had been stuck in the mud and muck for days. I yelled for Dad to get the vet. Most of the cows were already dead, including my Mother Cow and her four calves. Out of a herd of sixty cows, we were able to save only a few. I looked at Dad with hate in my heart. I said, "All this death was for nothing," I yelled. "Your carelessness brought this on. These calves were going to be my college money. Are you going to reimburse for my cows since this was your mistake?

"No," he replied, "I lost more cows than you did."

"But this was my college money!" I wailed. "You should reimburse me because this was clearly your mistake. It never needed to have happened."

Dad's face got red. "You forget about going to college," he said. "You're too stupid anyhow. Nobody in this family goes to college. We're all too stupid. Look what it did for my brother! He's nothing but a lazy, good-for-nothing piece of cow manure. Drop the idea now, Mary Jo. You're just too stupid."

I lifted my chin. "I will go to college someday. And I will do well. And I will graduate. You're not going to cheat me. The worst is that you killed Mother Cow. I hate you for that. You had no right to take her from me." I was livid with anger.

Dad ran to me and slammed his fist into me, knocking me

down in the mud close to Mother Cow. He left me there, sobbing. I said, "Jesus, this is more than I can bear! I don't like it down here. Sometimes I wonder why you don't stop my heart from beating. It is so broken! I just want to be with you! I keep losing everything down here that is precious to me."

The vet picked up a truckload of cows and left. The vet was to come back in the morning and pick up the rest of the dead cows. I asked him if he could load up the other cows so I could have one more day with her. The vet nodded yes. Then I said to Jesus, "You could bring her back. You did it for Lazarus; You could do it for Mother Cow. I would be forever grateful! Please!" I looked at Mother Cow, and she still did not move. I said to Jesus, "You don't want to, do You? Well, I'm not leaving her!" I stayed with Mother Cow until the roar of the veterinarian truck early the next morning woke me up. "I'll never forget you," I whisper into her ear. "I'll miss you every day." I thanked the vet for being gentle with Mother Cow.

I couldn't move from that spot. I sat down looking at the hole Mother Cow had been in and finally said to Jesus, "I don't know how to let go." I slumped to the ground. The vet stopped in town and told the townsfolk about what had happened to the cows. "Mary Jo looks like death, and there is no one to help her get through this."

Martha said, "We need to get up there now!"

Matthew, her husband, said, "Now, hold on a minute. Everybody is scared to go up there. They might kick us out before we could begin to search. We need someone to go there that has been there before."

Martha said, "Let's call Sharon, Mary Jo's friend in Low Ville."

They got Sharon on the phone and told her what had happened. Sharon told her dad, and her dad gave Sharon a ride to the farm. Sharon asked Zelda if she knew where I was. Zelda said she had no idea—there was no telling what no-good troublemaker was doing.

"I'll find her," Sharon said. She methodically looked in every building until all were searched with no sign of me. Sharon started praying, "Jesus, help me find her." Sharon got a thought; maybe I had never made it back. Sharon ran into the field toward the back pasture. Finally, Sharon saw me slumped to the ground. Sharon woke me up and helped me back to the house. I drank water like I was dying of thirst.

Sharon said, "You could have died out there, Mary Jo!"

I said, "So? Did you see what happened out there? Mother Cow is dead, and I am dead!"

Sharon started crying and said, "Can't you live for Jesus and the rest of us? We need you too!"

I started to talk several times but finally said okay. Jesus was teaching me to live for Him, putting Him first. Sharon gave me a huge hug, so relieved.

I learned that day to appreciate what you have today because you may not have it tomorrow. I still had Jesus, Bobby Dean, and Anna Kate. She would be back in mid-August.

My friend Sharon helped me to focus on other things. Sharon's mother advised me not to let Anna Kate see me grieving all the time. "She needs you to be stable and strong." I thank God for Sharon's family. They showed me how a loving family supports one another when tragedy strikes.

By the end of summer, Sharon's family was treating me like Sharon's twin sister. I worked and stayed with Sharon's family for six weeks after I lost Mother Cow. Every time I looked at the pasture, I wept.

Every day I continued to get stung by the bumblebees in the cornfields. One day when I went into the outhouse I heard bumblebee noises while I was doing my business. I hurried out of there. I said, "Sharon, I'm hearing bumblebees in there!" Sharon, waiting outside, laughed at me. "You're getting bumblebee phobia," she said, laughing as she stepped inside and shut the door. I waited for her. In a minute or two I heard screams. "Mary Jo! Mary Jo! Open the door!" she cried.

Three bumblebees were circling her on the pot with her pants down. "Stay still," I ordered. "I'll swat 'em so they'll come after me. Hit the dirt after I swat."

I took my hat off. As soon as I smacked at the bees with it they came after me like lightning. I ran faster than ever, but they traveled right along, buzzing around my ears. I dove into the dirt right in front of the forewoman, who swatted them away. I jumped two feet into the air and yelled, "I outran the doggone bumblebees!"

"Brown," my forewoman said, "get back to work." But I could see that she was having a hard time suppressing a smile. I ran back to Sharon, and we high-fived. I was pumping fists and saying, "Yes!" I was so happy that I remained on a high for the rest of the day. Sharon told her mother about the experience, and we all laughed until we almost make ourselves sick.

The summer ended, as it always does, and I collected the rest of the cornfield money. When Anna Kate returned from Oklahoma, we went shopping for clothing. We had enough money leftover to buy a used sewing machine at a great bargain after purchasing our school clothes. I even saved twenty dollars for an emergency.

Anna Kate had made wonderful new friends in Oklahoma and had flourished in the good environment. She looked more beautiful than ever. Boy, did Zelda notice! Her looks of hatred toward Anna Kate scared me.

"She has an evil grin on her face," Anna Kate told me one day.

"Ignore it," I told my sister. "Whatever she has planned won't work because Jesus will give us the strength to overcome it."

When my sister asked where Mother Cow was I explained what had happened. We cried together. Anna Kate asked, "You still miss them, don't you?" I answered, "Every single day!" We talked about Mother Cow for a long time. Anna Kate asked, "Do you think that Zelda talked him into bulldozing that day?" I answered, "I don't think I will ever know. I will miss her every day for the rest of my life! I still have you, and I thank God for that, and if it was Zelda, I pray that she cannot kill anyone else that I love." We hugged each other for a long time.

For the Want of a Book ...

Zelda's brother, Terry, came to live with us in late spring. Terry worked on the farm with Dad. Terry took a real liking to Anna

Kate. Terry took me and Anna Kate to the grocery store and other places. Once he drove us into the big city of St. Joseph, Missouri, and bought Anna Kate an outfit. I was happy that she could have a nice outfit for once.

Anna Kate and I registered for school the first week of September. We asked Dad to pay for the book fees of twenty dollars for each of us. "Zelda will write the check," he said.

"We're not paying the book fees this year," she told us.

She had written out the checks, but she ripped them up. When we told Dad, he looked in the checkbook, saw the entries, and accused us of lying. At school, we told them we were not given the money. The school called our house, and Zelda took the call. She told the authorities that she had given us the money. "If they won't pay for the books, Mary Jo will just have to drop out," she said.

Now I knew that she had been plotting this all along. She knew how much I loved school. Having to drop out would be devastating! I put down the twenty-dollars emergency money saved over the summer to pay half the book fees. The school clerks said they needed the other half in one week—at the latest.

We were desperate. We had to keep our promise and not contact Grandma. I asked everyone I knew. No one had money to lend. Sharon's family had put me up for the summer, free of charge. They had eight kids and could barely keep enough groceries in the house.

Anna Kate and I thought of asking Terry to find our mother in St. Joseph, Missouri, and taking us to see her. We never knew if he said yes because he liked Anna Kate so much or that he didn't like what his sister was doing. Terry called information and wrote down her telephone number and called her. Our mother wanted us to visit, so Terry took us on the next weekend. Mom seemed nice. She cussed her son of a female dog every other word and had a hard liquor bottle in her purse. It had been a month since visiting Mom. I prayed and prayed for a way to get the book money.

In desperation, I wrote to my mother in St. Joseph, Missouri, asking her to send twenty dollars. She agreed, provided I promise to live with her my final year of high school. She didn't care if Anna

Kate lived with her—just me. I talked it over with Anna Kate. We were so desperate. Anna Kate didn't think Mother would hold us to it, so she urged me to accept the offer. The money came right away. Zelda could never figure out how we got the money. She seemed frustrated that we were both going to school together as usual. Zelda was determined to find out how we got the money for the book fees. Zelda asked Terry if he had given us the money. Terry said no. Zelda wouldn't stop asking questions. She finally asked, "Do you know how they got the money?" Terry would not lie and Zelda knew it. Terry said yes.

"How did they get the money?" Zelda yelled.

Terry answered, "Their mother."

Zelda was shocked and furious. She said, "Their mother? How did they find her?"

Terry said, "I found her for them."

Zelda was beyond furious calling him a traitor and just about every other name in the book. Terry was gone the next morning. We never saw Terry again.

That year, our high school offered IQ tests. About a month afterward a counselor phoned me for an appointment. I went to his office at the appointed time and watched him go over my tests.

"I am not allowed to give you your IQ scores," he said, "but I am not happy with your grades. You should be making straight As."

"What are you talking about?" I asked. "I have been making close to a B average. That's very good for my family. My brother is nearly flunking. My dad says we are stupid, not good enough to go to college."

The counselor looked at me. "Normally, I don't give a range that your score is in because a lot of kids would brag to others. But I think you are an exception. I'm telling you that your test scores came out very high, just below the genius level."

I stared at him in total disbelief. "I don't believe it," I said flatly. "All Dad has ever told us all our lives is how stupid we are. Are you making this up so we'll work harder?"

"No," the counselor replied. "I am not making this up. Your dad never used the brains he had, or he wouldn't be talking like that. He is wrong!"

I hesitated. "Are you saying that I'm smart enough to go to college?"

He smiled. "Not only are you smart enough to go to college, you are smart enough to make As and Bs if you work hard."

Finally, my dream of going to college seemed attainable. I held on to that desperately during the last year in Kansas.

A Lesson Learned

One evening I overhead Zelda tell Dad how she had ironed the fifteen shirts that I had ironed the day before. I became so angry that I decided not to iron any of his shirts again. Let Zelda iron them if she was going to take credit for it.

One day Dad mentioned to Zelda that the shirts were piling up. "Better iron them soon," he said.

Sharon was spending the day with me. Zelda told me to iron the shirts. "No," I told her. "I heard you tell Dad that you ironed them, so you can just iron them all."

"You iron these shirts now!" Zelda yelled.

"No," I repeated. "If you want to take credit for the work then you can just do it yourself!"

Zelda became so angry she left and went into the kitchen. Sharon and Anna Kate looked at each other, wondering what was going to happen now. In half a minute, Zelda returned with a big pancake turner and started hitting me on the left front shoulder area. I stood there, not defending myself. Soon blood was flying everywhere because she kept beating me. Anna Kate and Sharon grabbed Zelda's arm, screaming at her to stop. Then we all three ran upstairs where Anna Kate and Sharon tried to stop the flow of blood. Anna Kate was angry with me, telling me I had too much pride to defend myself. "I need you to stay strong to help me get through this last year," she said.

The word pride that Anna Kate had said had hit me between the eyes. Had I been prideful? I had seen that word in the Bible so many times. My math teacher Mrs. Dodd noticed the wounds on my neck even though we tried to hide them. She called me into her office and said, "Everybody in this part of Kansas knows you are in a bad situation. I see the bruises on your neck and who knows where else. I am thinking about talking to your dad and stepmother."

I said, "It won't do any good. I made a mistake that caused the bruises, and I won't be making it again. You can't help us; nobody down here can. My sister's life depends on us not being separated. I am so grateful for all of you teachers. I hope Jesus blesses each and every one of you. Jesus is protecting us. He is the only one who can, and He is doing a mighty fine job if I say so myself."

Mrs. Dodd said, "If I see bruises like that again, you and I are going to the principal together."

I said, "You won't be seeing them again. I learned my lesson. Just know that I appreciate you!"

Mrs. Dodd said, "And another thing, don't you believe your dad about how stupid you are. It's nothing but a bunch of baloney."

I smiled at Mrs. Dodd and said, "You are so awesome!" and walked to my next class.

"You're always the wise one," I told my sister and ironed all the shirts that evening. Months later, Anna Kate overheard Zelda telling Dad that she had ironed the shirts that I had ironed.

"Does it bother you that Zelda is taking credit for it?" she asked me.

"Anna Kate, Jesus knows that I did the work," I said. "She may fool Dad, the people at church, and our neighbors, but she can't fool Jesus. He knows who did the work, and that's good enough for me."

Anna Kate smiled. "Mary Jo, you are getting wiser every day."

"Thanks for helping me get over that hurdle in life," I said as I gave her a big hug.

My cat became pregnant somehow and had kittens. My cat was gray with some black and white mixed in. She had six kittens—one was white, four were gray, and one was pure black. Zelda kept staring at the black cat. We knew the kitten was as good as dead as soon as she left the house.

Zelda's superstitions were very real to her, and she believed in them. The kitten disappeared as soon as it left the house. Zelda believed it could bring bad luck if it ran across the road in front of someone.

One morning, Anna Kate and I were cleaning house in our usual way when Zelda came rushing into the house demanding that we wash the windows immediately. I looked at my sister and shrugged. "You go ahead and finish. I'll wash the windows."

With rag and cleaner I went around the house outside, washing windows as I went. Someone had left a ladder standing up after working on our roof. I casually walked under it and kept washing windows.

Suddenly I heard laughter behind me. It sounded like an evil laugh, growing louder and louder. I turned and saw Zelda standing there. "Why are you laughing?" I asked. "Nobody's here."

She looked at me and smiled. I asked again what she was laughing at.

"Walking under a ladder is seven years' bad luck, but I believe it means you are doomed for the rest of your life." Suddenly I realized why she was so intent on my washing the windows. She had spotted the ladder and wanted to cast a spell on me.

"Your superstitions have no power over me," I told her calmly. "God is with me everywhere I go. He loves me. Show me in the Bible where it's wrong to walk under a ladder, and I'll agree I committed a sin against God. Until then, keep your superstitions to yourself. It's hogwash."

Then Zelda said emphatically, "You have days to live! I can take you out in thirty seconds."

I looked hard at Zelda and said, "My Jesus, the almighty God is in control down here, and if He says I go, you can get 'er done in two seconds. But if He says I stay, then nothing you try to do will take me out."

Zelda said, "Your Jesus has no control over me. I'm taking you out, and I will inherit this farm and everything the Browns' have ever owned."

I shook my head, saddened. I thought, "She is heaping burning coals on her head. You know what is the saddest thing, Jesus? It's that it could have been me! I was the one not long before saying, 'I don't need any God telling me what to do.' I was showing no respect for You at all. Praise You, Jesus, that You are the Lord of my life and have been for a long time! It was the best decision I ever made!"

I finished cleaning that window and washed the others around the house until they were all done. Then I headed upstairs to tell Anna Kate about the ladder curse. We both shook our heads, unable to understand Zelda's viciousness and superstitions. Later in the evening while I was reading the Bible, Anna Kate said, "Have you read anything about walking under ladders?"

I said, "Nope, I have read all the New Testament and part of the Old Testament and haven't seen anything so far."

Anna Kate said, "I didn't think so because it's not there!"

Bobby Dean had a cat as well. Bobby Dean's cat was totally white. Bobby Dean thought his cat was much prettier since my cat was speckled gray and unfortunately had ringworm. We had our cats for years, and they were doing well on the farm, catching mice and hissing and clawing at stray animals. One day, after a big rain that stopped all the farm work, Bobby Dean said to me, "Your cat is ugly!"

I said, "Are you calling my cat ugly?"

Bobby Dean said, "Yep."

I said, "Your cat is ugly!" and I quickly slapped his cat and took off running into the house. Thunder was behind me. Zelda had just waxed the kitchen floor, and it was slick. I ran as fast as I could and turned to the right at the kitchen sink barely making the turn. The next thing I heard was a crash into the sink. Bobby Dean had reached his arm out to grab my cat's tail and smashed into the sink. Bobby Dean's arm had a bone sticking up almost breaking the skin. It looked bad. Grandma Brown and Dad did not believe in doctors or any shots. I called for Grandma and she said, "It will heal."

I said, "Grandma, I've read about this in the library. His arm will haunt him the rest of his life if he doesn't get it set by a doctor.

We argued and discussed this for about thirty minutes. Grandma finally said, "Mary Jo, do you feel any guilt that you caused this?"

I said, "Slightly, but there was no need for name callin'!" looking over at Bobby Dean. I said, "Grandma, I won't let go until Bobby Dean goes to the doctor and gets the bone in a cast."

Grandma finally sighed and said, "Okay, let's go now."

The doctor took x-rays. The x-rays showed one bone fine and the other one completely broken. Bobby Dean had to keep his arm in the cast for six weeks and then his arm would be as good as new. Bobby Dean never called my cat ugly again, and I never smacked his cat again.

Longing for Heaven

Anna Kate asked me what I thought it would be like in heaven. "I think it's going to be more wonderful than we can ever imagine," I replied. "I'm looking forward to seeing Jesus. I don't know what I'm going to say to Him exactly, except: 'Thank You!'"

"Mary Jo, have you ever thought of going up there now so we could get away from all the bad down here? It would be wonderful, not like down here."

I looked at my sister, and my heart broke. She had suffered so much. "I thought of going up there when I was at the top of the tree. It was so peaceful up there. I got a taste that day of how wonderful it will be to see Jesus. But if He wanted us up there, He could take us in a heartbeat. I'm not going up there until He takes me. I don't want Jesus to have to ask me, 'Why did you end your life? Why didn't you believe in me enough to trust me?' No, I'm staying right here. You know, Anna Kate, today is just a moment in time. Some day we will have peaceful lives. I see it. We need to be patient. In a few months we can leave and be with Grandma and Freda May again. We can make a difference down here for Jesus. Our lives can help others. Do you understand what I mean?"

Anna Kate agreed. From then on, we talked only about what we were planning to do on this earth for the rest of our lives.

One day after stopping Zelda from beating up on Anna Kate, I sat in my cherry tree sobbing. "Jesus, I admit it. I would like to wipe Zelda out. Stomp her and my dad into the ground until there is nothing left but blood. You have made me strong enough that I could do it, too. They are evil! I know I am grieving you when I am justifying killing them. I know that I am talking about murder. I want to honor you more than taking them out even though I would like to pound them into the ground. Okay, I will give them to you to judge. I won't touch them. I give you my word. I will give them to you and trust you know best. Jesus, can you end the beatings soon and give us peaceful lives? How I long for it. When Grandma read me 1 Corinthians 10:13, it touched me. You are stronger than Zelda and her evil ways. I won't have any peace until I see Freda May again and tell her how sorry I am that I gave her a black eye. Jesus, give me the strength to wait."

I continued to take piano lessons and had become quite accomplished. Mrs. Pope had recitals every June. Mrs. Pope didn't know it, but this was going to be the last one I would be able to play.

Zelda's Hatred Continues

Zelda repeatedly told Anna Kate and me that we would inherit nothing.

"I'll personally make sure you get nothing," Zelda told us. Zelda asked Dad to write a will giving everything to her. Dad went to his lawyer the next week and had a will made up giving everything to Zelda. I learned a lesson in greed that day and prayed to God that Anna Kate and I could avoid this. Dad and Zelda seemed to be terribly messed up. We kept praying that God would rid them of hate and that we could leave soon. It had been over three years living with her and that seemed like an awfully long time.

Meanwhile, we had to endure our personal hell. Zelda's hatred for Anna Kate increased. I had to be with her all the time when Zelda was close. I needed to be doubly careful now as Zelda would drive back from the fields at unusual times just trying to find Anna Kate alone.

The next spring, I planted a garden as I had always done so Zelda would not suspect that we were planning to leave as soon as school was out. I planted the usual big garden with mostly vegetables. I had built up the soil with cow manure over the years so everything grew lightning fast. By May, I had planted everything and was harvesting onions, radishes, and carrots.

In the middle of May, at school, I wrote Mom a letter and asked if we could go down to Oklahoma to be with Freda May and Grandma. I explained that I had not seen them in years and did not wish to be separated from Anna Kate. I told Mom that the situation with Dad and Zelda had been bad for several years and that we sisters wanted to stay together.

"I'll work and pay you one hundred dollars [five times the twenty dollars borrowed] if you will let me stay with Grandma and my sisters. Write me back at Sharon's address," I requested.

About a week later, Sharon handed me a letter from Mom. I hugged it to my breast and raised my eyes in prayer, hoping for the best. With Anna Kate and Sharon sitting with me at recess, I read the letter.

"I expect you to keep your word," she said. "No amount of money can replace you coming to live with me. Anna Kate can come, too, if she wants to."

We all cried. Anna Kate and I talked over our options. She could come with me, but she wanted to go to Oklahoma. No telling what situations we would run into with Mom. So we decided that Anna Kate would go to Oklahoma, and no amount of persuasion from Anna Kate could cause me to break my promise to Mom. Before God I had to keep my word. So Anna Kate would go to Oklahoma, and I would go to St. Joseph, Missouri, for one year. I hated the thought of giving up my sister for a whole year, especially since I hadn't seen my other sister for over three years by then. It was the hardest decision of my life—so hard that I went and sat in my cherry tree, asking Jesus for the strength to let her go. I couldn't do it. I wanted to keep Anna

Harvesting Hope

Kate with me at all costs, even if it was a better situation for her in Oklahoma. I told Jesus how selfish I felt. I had already lost Freda May; I was not going to lose Anna Kate, too.

Oklahoma was clearly the best place for my little sister. She would be taken care of and not beaten up all the time. Why couldn't I just think of her and not be so selfish?

"I don't like Mom making you keep your promise, Mary Jo," Anna Kate said. "You don't have to go to her house. It's not like she kept any promises to us. She left us and didn't even care about us enough to visit us."

"I know, Anna Kate," I said. "It's hard for me, too. But it's right for me to keep my word. I'm not keeping my word to impress Mom or anybody else. I am going to St. Joseph because I made the promise, and I have to live up to it. It scares me to live in the big city. There are thousands of people living there. All I care about is that you are in a better situation. Grandma and Freda May will take good care of you. That means everything to me. Jesus will be with me. Besides, it's only for a year."

I told her Jesus was in control. He knew this was going to happen. It would be all right. I would be graduating from high school next year and would be on track to go to college.

"Let's not talk about it anymore," I suggested. "Let's focus on enjoying each other every day. We need to figure out what we will be taking with us later this month. We can leave the rest."

We began carefully sorting out our clothes in our closets. On the left we put clothes we planned to take with us; on the right we put clothes we would leave behind. And when I prayed that night, I thanked Jesus for giving me the strength to let my sister go. I was amazed because I had been so determined not to be separated from Anna Kate. I had missed Freda May too much and thought separation from both sisters would be too much to bear. But Jesus gave me strength not only to say good-bye but know that I could put my sister on that bus with total hope that Jesus would take care of her until the day I would see her again. That hope gave me a peace that I had never had before.

One day in the middle of May, Anna Kate was washing dishes and cleaning up the house when I said I was going to go out to the garden and see if a weed had sneaked in. First I looked out the window and made sure Zelda was still working far out in the last eighty acres with Dad. It was safe for me to leave Anna Kate alone.

After filling a small basket with radishes, carrots, pea pods, and an onion, I headed for the house, feeling good about how perfect my garden was. When I opened the door I heard fighting. Then I saw Zelda slugging Anna Kate and my sister hitting back.

"Stop!" I yelled, but Zelda hit Anna Kate again. I ran toward Zelda like lightning.

This enraged Zelda so much she grabbed her two-by-four and hit me with it when she saw me coming, but the wood bounced off my shoulder and flew into a different room. Zelda and I started fighting and pushing each other. Zelda tried to push me down, but I had grown strong enough to push back with even more force than she had. She kept trying to punch me, but I punched back and was getting the better of the fight for once. Then I grabbed her by the shoulders and pushed forward and down with all my strength. She lost her balance. I pushed her forward, and she hit the wall with her head and sank to the floor, squirming and moaning.

"Oh," Zelda moaned, "I can't get up."

"I hate all this fighting," I said to Zelda, "but you're not touching Anna Kate again. Keep your filthy hands off of her, or you'll be dealing with Jesus and me."

Zelda moaned that I had tried to kill her. Anna Kate had witnessed everything and was afraid for me. "Dad may kill you for this," she said.

I looked down at Anna Kate but said nothing. I heard a noise and was shocked to see Dad walking through the front door in the middle of the afternoon. He usually stayed out in the fields until dark.

"Get back," I told Anna Kate. "No telling what's going to happen now."

Dad went over to Zelda and asked what had happened. She told him Anna Kate and I had tried to kill her and that we were rotten kids. Zelda told him to beat the crap out of us.

"She's a liar!" I told Dad. "I came in and found her beating up Anna Kate again. She took a two-by-four and hit me with it. Just look in the next room. It took me a while, but I finally got the best of the fight. Anna Kate has been beat up too much! You might look good on Sunday to the people in church and might even fool your neighbors, but Jesus sees what is going on here. Jesus knows Anna Kate is getting beat up too much just like you and I know. Anyone who tries to beat her up is going to have to get through me first, and Jesus will give me the strength to stop it."

Anna Kate noticed the kitchen wall cabinets were behind me. They went from the ceiling to about four-and-a-half feet above the floor. If I got hit and sent backward, the back of my neck could hit the cabinets. Anna Kate was really scared now and was calling out to Jesus to protect me.

I lifted my chin to show Dad I meant business. Dad curled his tongue in anger as he had done many times before when he hit me, but this time he did not. He just stared at me and then at Zelda for a few minutes. Then he walked to his bedroom. No one could believe it. Zelda screamed for him to come back to help her up, but Dad just kept on walking.

It was a miracle! Anna Kate and I grabbed some food and headed upstairs. We didn't come down until the next day. I asked Anna Kate what had started the fight. "Zelda came into the house and immediately came over to me and called me her favorite prostitute name," my sister explained. "Usually I say nothing when she does that; this time I couldn't take it and told her, 'It takes one to know one.'"

Zelda had flown into a rage, calling my sister more names and starting to beat her. I opened the door just in time to stop the altercation.

"Sometimes I hate Zelda for beating on you," I said. "Sometimes I want to smash her into the earth and wipe her out, then at other times I feel sorry for her because she's so messed up. Crazy situation, huh?"

"Don't ever wipe her out, Mary Jo," my sister said. "She's not worth your life. We need to pray for strength to overcome the hate because God would never want us to kill her. It's right in front of our faces in the Ten Commandments." Anna Kate didn't know how I had been tempted so many times. I kept reading Matthew 5:21: "You have heard that it was said to the people long ago, 'Do not murder and anyone who murders will be subject to judgment.'" I wanted Jesus's favor, so I knew I had to obey no matter how tempting.

"Anna Kate," I said, "you have always been so wise. I'm blessed to have you."

We thanked God together and prayed to Jesus, His Son, for His guidance and that He had protected us.

I stayed up late one night deliberately planning to say good-bye to Bobby Dean. I hugged him and talked to him like I would never see him again. Bobby Dean said, "You act like you may never see me again!" I replied, "Do we know anything anymore? Did we know that we would not see Grandma and Freda May? It's been years now. I just want you to know how much I love you!" We talked until we got so tired we both went to bed.

The Great Escape

Two weeks were left of school, so we began to plan how we would get away. But how to contact Grandma? How could we let her know Anna Kate would be coming to live with her? Sharon invited Anna Kate and me to come to her house that weekend and lay out our plans. Dad and Zelda were in the middle of planting corn and said it would be okay as long as we could get a ride from someone.

"Sharon, we need to talk to Grandma to see if she could send us bus money, but Anna Kate and I gave our word that we wouldn't call Grandma," I said. Sharon smiled and said, "I didn't promise."

Sharon called collect to Oklahoma and the operator connected her to Grandma. We took turns talking to her. "Anna Kate can come down. I'll send the bus money for you to get to St. Joseph, Missouri, and for Anna Kate to get here," Grandma said. I told her I would call her from there to tell her where I was going to be. It was so good to talk to Grandma again. I asked if Freda May was there, but she was not.

The money for the bus fare came to Sharon's house right on schedule. I bought the bus fares and kept them in Sharon's room at her house. Anna Kate and I began sneaking things out of the house and storing them in Sharon's home until we left. The larger things went out in an old suitcase we found that last day we went to school. Sharon took everything to her house at lunchtime.

After school that day we didn't take the bus home. We went instead to Sharon's house to separate our clothes and get Anna Kate to the bus station. I didn't know how hard it would be to see her go. I felt as though I was losing part of myself. I told her how much I was going to miss her.

"It doesn't seem right that you have to be alone now with the rest of us in Oklahoma," Anna Kate said.

"I'll never be alone," I told my sister. "I have Jesus with me everywhere I go. He is in control and knows what is going to happen. I can be strong and wait until next June to join all of you. God knows that I won't stop until I can see Freda May again. I'm trusting Jesus to take care of you until I can come down there in June after graduation."

Suddenly the bus was there to take Anna Kate to Oklahoma. We loaded on her one suitcase, cried, hugged, and waved good-bye. I stood for a long time watching that bus travel down the road. So Anna Kate went to Oklahoma to live with Freda May and Grandma, and I went to live with our real mother. So began our separate lives.

Sharon and I looked for a telephone stand. We had two hours before my bus arrived, and we needed to call Grandma and let her know that Anna Kate was on the bus. When I spoke with Grandma, she told me that Freda May was out with friends. "She's looking forward to seeing you next year," Grandma told me.

And then it was time to leave Sharon's house for my bus. Again I cried because of the separation from a dear friend. "I won't be far away," I told Sharon, "and I'll miss you."

As I rode that bus to Missouri, I talked to God. I told Him that

I never thought I'd be without my siblings. "But I know you are in control, Jesus," I prayed, "Even though I don't always understand the things that are happening. I believe you, and I trust you. Take care of my sisters and Grandma. Holy Spirit, give me wisdom and peace in St. Joseph."

For the first time in my life, I felt the pain of being totally separated from the family I love. The heavenly Father was separated from His Son, Jesus. Not only did God suffer from the separation, He watched His only Son die for us to remove sin for all time. I would never let one of my sisters die to save the world. I just couldn't do it. I just don't love the world that much. But the almighty God is an awesome God to love us that much. I told Jesus, "I know my mother will not be a friend. She's just too messed up. I'm just glad that I have you."

The bus made it to St. Joseph, and my mother was there to meet me. I hardly recognized her. She looked rough. She had her hair in pink sponge curlers. She had a cigarette in her mouth and a bottle of liquor in her purse. When she talked, she said "son of a female dog" every other word. I had to be very careful of anything I said because any little thing could start conflict with her.

Chapter 5

LIFE WITH MOTHER

The Lord your God is with you, he is mighty to save.
He will take great delight in you. He will quiet you
with His love. He will rejoice over you with singing.

—Zephaniah 3:17 (NIV)

Senior Year in High School

Mother took me to her home, which was a small house that my stepdad had inherited. Mother and Stepdad seemed happy that I was there and were overall pretty good to me. They both drank every day after work. Stepdad seemed to change jobs every month. He had a variety of skills: repairing vehicles, driving trucks, working at filling stations, handyman jobs. Mother worked as a waitress, janitor, and at other unskilled jobs. Bill collectors called just about every day. I learned quickly that Mother and Stepdad were writing hot checks all over the place, staying just one step ahead of them. They bought me a few school clothes. They could not buy me five outfits, so I would need to wash them every other day.

Mom was too unstable to become my friend. That made me lonely. She told me she didn't have the money to call Grandma and my sisters in Oklahoma and that I couldn't call them collect. I hadn't felt that lonely before or ever since that time. One night I prayed, "God, I know You're always with me, and I thank You for that. It's just that I'm so lonely down here. I don't have any friends, and You know Mom's too messed up to be a friend. Sometimes I just wish Jesus were back down here with me. I know He'd rather be up there where everything is so nice. I'm just mighty thankful that You love me and will watch over me." I felt good telling Jesus how lonely I'd been and asking Him for a friend.

After a week or so I asked Mom if I could go to work that summer to pay for my own clothes. She and Stepdad thought that was a great idea. Mom knew of an opening for a dishwasher at the truck stop a few miles away. She drove me to the truck stop the next day. They needed a dishwasher for Saturdays and Sundays from 7:00 a.m. to 3:00 p.m. The job paid only one dollar per hour, but that seemed like a lot to me.

I started working the next weekend. Grandma Patterson was selling her 1958 Chevy for two hundred dollars. Mom loaned me the money so I could drive myself to work and back. I paid Mom twenty dollars a week so I'd have the car paid off by the time school started.

The work was enjoyable and everyone was good to me. The cooks would make me meals and chat with me while I worked. When anyone called in sick on the evening shift during the week, they would ask me to work it first.

On the second Saturday of work I became thirsty. I went out front to get a soft drink and met a male truck driver in his forties. "Hi," he said, and I answered with the same greeting. "I haven't seen you before. Are you new here?" he asked.

"Yes, I started just last week."

The truck driver asked, "Can you talk for a minute without getting into trouble?"

I looked around for a second because I didn't really know. The waitress heard the question and came over. "Look," she told me, "you can talk for ten minutes every morning and afternoon if you want. You do such a great job that you can take a break and still get your work done."

"Thanks," I said. "You're so nice."

The waitress laughed. "Enjoy yourself, and take a break."

So I kept visiting with the truck driver who was running to California and back. The trip took five days, so he had part of Saturday, Sunday, and Monday to be with his family. Every Saturday he stopped at this truck stop on his way to Kansas City, Missouri. He had two boys and a girl, and he told me how much fun they were. I told him how I had just moved from Kansas over to St. Joseph and that I was living with my mother. "Do you get lonely driving out on that road away from your family every week?" I asked.

"Yes, but it pays well. It helps if you have friends along the way. Would you be my friend?"

"Yes," I said.

"My name's Joe. I'll be coming through here every Saturday morning. See you next week," he said.

Joe smiled at me as I said, "My name is Mary Jo. I'll be looking forward to seeing you." That night when I prayed, I thanked God for giving me a friend when I needed one the most.

I always worked hard until the minute Joe got there. Joe would ask the waitress if I was back there. The waitress would tell him I was and that I hadn't stopped working all morning just waiting for him. She smiled and then yelled, "Mary Jo! Joe is here."

I'd hurry to get to a stopping point and barrel through the door. Joe started introducing me to other truck drivers. Some had their wives with them. They liked to tease me and tell jokes. They made me feel like I was part of their families.

After washing dishes for about a month I asked the waitress if she thought I could learn to be a waitress. "I think you would be a good waitress," she told me. "You just need to learn the menu and watch for a day or so. We're short two waitresses now. I could put in a good word for you."

"That would be great!" I said, giving her a hug. I'd get a 10 percent raise plus tips. That would help me pay off my car a lot faster.

A week later the manager of the restaurant talked to me about working as a waitress. "Would you like to try?" he asked. "We have two openings. You can have one if you will train for a couple of days."

I told him I'd love it. "When can I start?"

"How about next week?" When I accepted, he smiled. "There are going to be some people around here missing their good dishwasher," he said.

"Thanks," I told him. "You have been very kind to me. I'll work hard for you."

"I'm sure you will," the manager said.

I was put into training with the girl who had put in a good word for me. I memorized the menu and practicing taking orders and remembering the names of everyone who ordered. Memorizing names was the hardest part.

The next Saturday Joe was surprised to see me in a waitress uniform. "No one deserves it more than you," he said. I was moving to the 3:00 p.m. to 11:00 p.m. shift and wouldn't see him much. He said he would run late some Saturdays and still see me.

I loved being a waitress and gave the best service I could. When I wasn't busy I'd visit with customers and make friends. Soon I had customers who would sit only in my section. Truck drivers were especially good to me.

One night after work my car wouldn't start. Two of the truck drivers offered to take a look under the hood. They quickly saw what was wrong and fixed it. I paid only for the replacement part because they wouldn't take any money.

As truck drivers got to know me, they learned that I'd had a rough time growing up. They offered advice about boys, saving money, and planning for college. They treated me like a daughter and a special friend. Before I realized it, I had a whole bunch of friends, which made it so much fun to work at that restaurant.

By the first week in August I had the car paid for. With money to spare, I asked Mom if I could call my sisters. "I'd prefer that you not call them until next spring," she said. "Calling them will just make you want to leave here. And you know you start school in two weeks."

I was angry, but I said nothing. That night I prayed for strength to get over my anger. Just nine more months and I was heading to Oklahoma. No one could stop me then.

Boy, was city school different from the one in my small town in Kansas. Sharon, Carolyn, and I had buddied around all the time back home. Carolyn was black, but color didn't make any difference. You could pick anyone as your friend. I was totally naïve about race discrimination and couldn't understand it at all. One poor white girl told me the whites wouldn't accept me if I continued to be friendly to the blacks.

"Why?" I asked. "I don't understand."

"I don't know where you come from, but here whites stay with their own and blacks stay with theirs," she said, giving me a look like I must be mentally challenged or something.

I ignored her advice and continued to be friends with everyone of both races. But one day I rode to a basketball game with a group of classmates and sat next to a black boy and a white girl. We won the game that night, and all of us had a lot of fun. But rumors began flying that I was pregnant by the black boy I sat beside.

At the truck stop the next day I told Joe about the rumors at school. "Have I done something wrong?" I asked.

"No," he replied, "but you need to be careful about associating yourself with boys of a different race. People talk and think the worst. Back in Kansas people knew everything was clean, but here in the big city people do all sorts of things. Lay low for a while. Just spend time with girls. Are you interested in boys at all?"

"No, not at all," I said.

"Well," said Joe, "That makes it a lot easier right now. With rumors like that floating around, you very likely wouldn't find a decent one."

I thanked Joe for being such a good friend. I took his advice and concentrated on making girlfriends while being friendly to all the kids.

A nice boy of Philippine heritage named John told me after a basketball game, "Mary Jo, you are a real nice girl. I want you to know that I will marry you and say the baby is mine."

I looked at him with a puzzled expression. "What baby?"

"It's all over school that you are pregnant," he said.

"John, I appreciate your offer. That would be an enormous sacrifice on your part, and it shows how caring you are. But I'm not pregnant. I know this is hard for you to believe, but I've never had sex and don't intend to for a long time. I just have friends of every color."

I explained to John that I had an abusive father and stepmother, carried a huge chip on my shoulder against men, and avoided men because I didn't want anyone to pay for what my dad did—"especially a sweet man like you, John."

Coincidentally, I had been in a car wreck about four months earlier, and my body slammed into the dashboard. Afterward I didn't have any periods. Mom freely admitted to me that she had told several of my girlfriends at school that she thought I was pregnant, which clearly fueled the ugly rumor. I was humiliated. What kind of mother would tell your friends a piece of gossip like that without discussing the problem with her own daughter? My body finally recovered and everything got back to normal, but those rumors lingered my whole senior year.

The new school was a big adjustment, but I worked hard to keep my grades up to high C average. All through my senior year I worked at the truck stop. Joe brought me a Christmas gift that year. I had one for him, too. He took two weeks off to be with his family, so I didn't see him until January.

That week was a nasty one in Missouri, bringing lots of snow and sleet. I began to long for spring. One weekday in the first week in February Grandma Brown called me while I was doing homework. I was shocked to hear that she had returned to Kansas and was at her old house again.

"Why did you leave my sisters in Oklahoma?" I asked. "Who's taking care of them?"

"Hank Ray needed me," Grandma explained. "He's been in

trouble again. Besides, Freda May is taking care of Anna Kate. She's eighteen, you know."

I said, "Get him out of jail, and go back to Oklahoma." I still couldn't believe that Grandma would leave my sisters in Oklahoma. "They will fight, Grandma. Anna Kate will resent any control from Freda May because she's been through so much. Didn't Anna Kate tell you about it?"

"She never says anything about Kansas," said Grandma.

I said, "Grandma, didn't you even ask?"

Grandma said, "Mary Jo, you're hurting me. You act as though you won't be happy to see me, even though you haven't seen me for years."

"Grandma, I am very happy to even talk to you. I'll see you this Sunday, and we will be together again."

"I'm looking forward to seeing you," she said. "Don't worry about Freda May and Anna Kate. They'll be fine."

That night I prayed for my sisters. Only God and I knew what Anna Kate had gone through back home. I was shocked that Grandma didn't even ask. I told Jesus, "Nobody's going to know all the awesome things You have done to protect us! Nobody even asks!" I left my sisters in God's care and prayed they would both try to get along together.

A Baby for Sale

Mom and Stepdad kept changing jobs, always deep in financial problems. I took a phone call one evening while Mom was working. The caller stated that she had bought a baby girl from Mom a couple of years earlier and had heard through the grapevine that she was pregnant again. They gave me a phone number and asked that Mom call them.

That night Mom shocked me by admitting that it was true and that she was five months pregnant. "We needed the money," she said.

"Are you going to keep this baby?" I asked.

She answered that she thought she would.

Mom, messed up from disobedience and sin, told me incredible stories. Most of them didn't make sense. She would ramble on about how much she hated my dad and how she had been forced to marry him, but her wedding and family pictures show her smiling. It's sad to admit, but her actions become so outrageous and argumentative that I could not believe anything she said.

Financial problems in the home continued to escalate. Mom began to steal any cash she found in my room. And she stole the settlement to reimburse me for the medical expenses of the car accident I was in. I stopped cashing my paychecks until I needed the money, struggling to survive until June.

No Place like Home

Going home was like following the yellow brick road from the Land of Oz back to Grandma's house. Happy memories flooded my mind as I stepped inside her old house. I hugged her tight, and we talked for hours, catching up on everything. Grandma was such a sweetheart. I could tell her anything.

Uncle Hank Ray had begun living with Grandma again. His habits were grosser than before. He made the house look like a pigsty. Trash piled on newspapers lay everywhere. I could hardly find a place to sit down.

When I told Grandma about the situation with Mom, she invited me to stay with her and Uncle Hank Ray until I graduated.

"Thanks, Grandma," I said, "but I made a promise, and I will keep it. I'll be all right."

She told me all about Freda May and Anna Kate and where they were living, adding, "I'm coming to your high school graduation in May."

In May—only a few months away. It felt good to be almost there. I did my homework every Saturday and visited Grandma every Sunday from 4:00 p.m. to 9:00 p.m. Life was sweet with Grandma at my side, but what about my sisters? I was almost afraid to ask Grandma if she had talked with them since we last met.

Joe and other truck drivers would ask me how Grandma was. I asked Joe to pray for my sisters all alone in Oklahoma. Over time, I related to Joe all that happened in Kansas. "Hard to believe," he said, "but I'm more proud than ever to be your friend. Now I understand why you avoid having boyfriends. Are you afraid one will beat you up?"

"Yes!" I said. "I'm afraid of making the same mistake my mother did. Her dad would get drunk and beat up all the kids, so at seventeen she married my dad just to get away, not knowing he had a violent temper. My dad was a good-looking man. You can never tell who's going to be violent. But Joe, I'm going to college, so I really don't want to get married or anything for a long time—maybe never."

"Mary Jo, you are smart to concentrate on going to college. Let God pick your husband. If He wants you to have one, He'll put him right in front of your face."

"Joe, you are special," I told my friend. "You've helped me so much!"

"You're going to make it through high school and college. I see it."

"I see it too, Joe," I said.

Walking the Plank

I saved my money my senior year, and in the spring I decided to purchase a better car with a payment of eighty dollars per month. A couple of weeks before graduation I bought it. Boy, today I am sorry I sold that car because it was so special.

With graduation set for the end of May, Grandma took me shopping and bought me a pretty dress to wear. It was always so nice to spend time with Grandma. I thanked Grandma and gave her a big hug. Then I headed back to St. Josephs that night with my new dress. There was a lot of work to do to get ready for graduation.

"You look very nice," Mom told me when I tried on my new dress from Grandma.

Final examinations flew by, and graduation would be next week!

I went to work at the truck stop that weekend feeling so happy. When I finished my shift, I headed to Grandma Brown's house as usual. This time Grandma seemed to be a little bothered by something but was trying to hide it. I tried to make conversation and told her everyone likes my new dress. Finally, I asked Grandma, "What's wrong?"

"Well, Freda May and Anna Kate have been fighting badly," she confided. "Freda May says Anna Kate is full of hate and won't listen to anything she says. I got Anna Kate on the phone separately and heard Freda May puts too many demands on her She says she hates Freda May. They got into such a shouting match right on the phone°... it was awful."

"Grandma," I said, "it's no one's fault. You didn't know what torture Anna Kate went through with Zelda, or you wouldn't have left them down there. Anna Kate was too young to leave there. I should have taken her along to St. Joseph. I didn't because I knew Mom was such a mess."

Grandma and I cried together. "Mary Jo, you were right about the fighting. I made a mistake leaving them. I just hope they can get past this and be friends again someday."

I am sad to say that to this day they are not friends and don't speak to each other. Some people choose not to forgive and move on.

I suggested to Grandma that as soon as I graduate, the following week we should go down to Oklahoma and help straighten them out.

"Okay," she said, "but I'll need to check to see if it's all right with Hank Ray first.

"Grandma," I said, "I'm going whether Uncle Hank Ray likes it or not." We prayed that my sisters would come to an understanding and start getting along.

I passed all my finals that week and then took Saturday off to prepare for the graduation ceremony that afternoon. It was so exciting to walk across the platform to receive my high school diploma. I was so excited that I bought a high school ring that I still wear on my finger to this day. It meant so much to me, especially since I had to fight for it, that I have never taken it off and will be buried with it on.

Grandma whispered to me afterward, "I'll be looking forward to your next graduation, too."

I was so touched by her affirmation that a tear ran down my cheek. "Grandma," I said, "you see it, too, don't you?"

"Yes, I do," she replied.

I had fulfilled my promise to my mother, so my first order of business was to find my own place to live. After searching for several weeks, I found a tiny eight-by-thirty foot mobile house that I could rent for one hundred dollars per month. This would work fine for a while. In St. Joseph, I was driving distance from Grandma. I decided to drive to Oklahoma to see my sisters and then return to my mobile home and work full-time at the truck stop and do anything else I could to get ahead financially.

Chapter 6

REUNION

Your kingdom is an everlasting kingdom, and you dominion endures through all generations. The Lord is faithful to all his promises and loving toward all he has made. The Lord upholds all those who fall and lifts up all who are bowed down.

—Psalm 145:13, 14 (NIV)

After graduation on Saturday, I went to work on Sunday at the truck stop. My manager agreed to give me the following week off if I worked every day that week.

On Wednesday evening I was washing clothes and packing items for my trip when the telephone rang. Grandma was on the line.

"Mary Jo, can you come to my house tonight?" she asked.

"Sure," I replied. "Are you all right?"

"Yes, but it's important that you come here tonight. I'll be waiting. Can you come right away?"

"I'm on my way," I told Grandma.

I told Mom about the call and that I'd phone if I wasn't coming back that night. By driving fast I got to Grandma's house in record time. When I arrived, I ran up the stairs and opened the front door.

There stood Freda May. I gave her a big hug and told her how good it was to see her.

"I'm sorry for giving you that black eye and not appreciating you," I told my sister.

"Forget it," Freda May replied. "I didn't do everything right either."

I was so happy to see my sister that I began jumping up and down. I kept repeating, "Yes! Thank You, Jesus!" I think Freda May and Grandma thought I had lost it. "Zelda kept telling me I would never see Freda May again," I explained. "She was wrong, and I thank You, Jesus, for that." After I calmed down I took a close look at my eldest sister.

Freda May bowed her head and covered her eyes. "It's been a bad situation in Oklahoma," she told me. "Cliff was my boyfriend for more than a year. We were going to get married. He asked me to go to Washington State and meet his family. But when we got there, he started to spend time with an old girlfriend. I left and came here. I haven't heard a word since.

"To make matters worse," she went on, "Anna Kate and I developed a hateful relationship. Ever since Grandma left us to return here, Zelda's brother has taken over. He told Anna Kate that she didn't have to listen to me—that he would take care of her. I set a curfew of midnight, but she would stay out until one or two in the morning. She broke any rules I made. Our relationship deteriorated into shouting matches every time we talked to each other. The worst one was just last week. We actually tried to beat each other up. It was horrible." Freda May began to cry. Brad, Zelda's brother, had taken care of Anna Kate the summer before while I was working in the cornfields.

Grandma, sitting nearby, covered her face and wept. "I'll drive down to Oklahoma and talk to Anna Kate," I told my eldest sister. "Where are you planning to live now?"

"I don't know," Freda May replied. "I just want to start a new life somewhere."

"I do too," I said, "but we need to figure out where. We could go together. I will work for a month as many hours as I can get and save some money for the trip. I'll bet you could get a job around here. Let's plan to leave in a month or so."

"Sounds good to me," Freda May replied. "I was lost, but you always seem to know where you're going."

"Well, actually I don't right now," I admitted, "but I soon will. Let's pray about it and see where God leads us."

Arriving in St. Joseph after midnight I got to bed at one o'clock in the morning. The alarm rang at 6:15, so I was tired that day, but still okay to work. I worked long hours all week, including double shifts because some people called in sick. Finally it was time for me to head for Oklahoma to see Anna Kate. After packing my car and telling Mom I'd be back in approximately eight days, I drove to Grandma's house. Freda May looked a little better. She had cleaned the house—Grandma liked it, but Uncle Hank Ray did not! He kept complaining that Freda May threw out newspaper articles that he wanted to keep. "I don't like someone coming in here and changing everything," he growled. To Freda May he said, "I can see why Anna Kate doesn't like you." With a look of disgust he added, "You dominate everyone."

When Freda May started to cry I stepped up and said, "Uncle Hank Ray, you have no right to say those things. Freda May was put in a tough place trying to raise Anna Kate by herself. She wasn't ready for that responsibility. She did the best she could."

I looked around the room. "And besides, it's about time someone really cleaned up this pigsty. It hasn't been a healthy place for a long time. You complained about my cleaning, so don't act as though Freda May did something wrong. If you lose newspaper articles it's your own fault for not filing them."

Uncle Hank Ray grunted. "You're worse than Freda May!"

"Thank you for the compliment," I said. Freda May laughed.

Reunion with Baby Sister

Bright and early the next morning I headed for the Sooner State, arriving late in the day. Anna Kate put me in the back bedroom where I slept like a rock, waking up at ten the following morning. Roger, her boyfriend, had come over. Anna Kate introduced us. We talked about what had happened down there with Freda May and the hatred Anna Kate had for Freda May came spilling out.

"She's been so controlling," said my little sister, "that I'm glad she's gone." As my sister talked, Roger never said a word.

"You've been through so much, Anna Kate," I said. "Do you remember that Grandma asked Freda May to take care of you? That she was in charge? She was doing the best she could."

"Mary Jo, you weren't down here," she said, "so you don't know how bad she was. I don't want to see her for a lo-o-ng time."

"Come on, Anna Kate, let's forgive one another and move on. You know you didn't treat Freda May right all the time either. Remember how bad I was when I beat all of you up? You forgave me for that. You can forgive Freda May for any mistakes she's made down here, can't you?"

"It will take time, Mary Jo. It will take time."

"Okay," I said, "but pray about it. Jesus commands us to forgive others."

My week with baby sister went by rapidly, but we packed into it all we could. Anna Kate told me about her high school and what she had been doing. Roger announced proudly that he and Anna Kate were planning to be married as soon as she turned eighteen. I congratulated them both but wondered whether my sister knew herself well enough to make that life-changing decision.

We took walks together, went to the movies, and did some shopping. We also visited Roger's family and got acquainted with our new relatives-to-be. Then it was time to return to St. Joseph.

"You know how important it is to finish high school, don't you?" I asked Anna Kate.

"Yes, Mom," she answered with a smile. "I'll finish high school and with good grades."

I laughed. "I guess you got that soaked in pretty good," I said. "But you know, I'm having a hard time leaving you down here by yourself."

"I'll be fine, Mary Jo," Anna Kate replied. "I'm getting married soon, and I want to stay here."

"Okay. Just so you're happy. I can see that you want to stay here. I'll support you in any way I can. Call me if you need anything," I said. "I love you and will miss you."

We said our good-byes and then I headed back to Grandma's house, stopping for a few minutes to update Grandma and Freda May on my visit. Our sister's comment "It will take time" bothered Freda May. But it was so good to see both of my sisters inside a week. It gave me a peace I had not felt for so many years. I thanked God that night for bringing us together.

When I arrived at Mom's house she told me they were selling their little house. "That's all right," I told her. "I'm moving into a small mobile home."

I went to work the next morning and didn't see Mom very often after that. Mom had a baby boy. They decided to keep him. I wondered what kind of life the little boy would have with them, but I said nothing.

I worked as often as possible at the truck stop, sometimes all three shifts when needed. I even tried working two full-time jobs—one at a factory and one at the truck stop—but it was too much. As often as possible, I slipped away to visit Grandma and Freda May. Even while making car payments and paying rent I was able to save money.

One day I arrived at work about twenty minutes ahead of my three o'clock punch-in and saw so many of my precious friends. Joe was there with other friends at the trucker's table, telling them how he was going to take a two-week vacation to Disneyland with his family. During a lull in the conversation I told them, "I just wanted you all to know that my sister, Freda May, is at my grandma's house now. Grandma called me a week ago as a surprise, and there I saw my eldest sister for the first time in a long, long time.

"I got to tell her how sorry I was for giving her a black eye when we were kids," I said.

My friends all congratulated me. They seemed happy about my good fortune.

"You know," I continued, "God is faithful. I was tempted to hate and retaliate for all the bad stuff my stepmother did. She told me I would never get to talk to my sister again. God had mercy on me. I got to see both of my sisters in the last two weeks. I am so thankful! Now I have a new life and have escaped the bad memories of my childhood. But I need your help."

When I said that, all eyes turned to me and everyone waited for me to continue.

"My sister, Freda May, dated a guy down in Oklahoma for about a year. They were going to get married, so he took her to Washington State to meet his folks. But up there he met up with his old girlfriend and left Freda May. She was heartbroken. My sister and I are thinking of moving somewhere together to start a new life. Grandma thinks it should be at least five hundred miles from here so Mom can't interfere with our lives. Where do you think we should live?"

There was quiet talk around the table for a few minutes. "Well," Joe began, "the safest city I can think of for two single ladies is Salt Lake City. It's very different, but it's safe."

Others nodded in agreement. I looked at the clock. "Gotta be at work in a minute. I don't think it was just luck you all are here today. I'll be leaving in a few days. You are special to me. You were my friends when I had no other friends here. You helped me to get through a very hard year." I paused and then added quietly, "I may never see you again, but you have all made me feel very special."

"Mary Jo, you are special," said Joe.

"I thank all of you for everything." I smiled. "Look, I need to get to work. I'm two minutes late already. If I'm not lucky enough to see any of you again, I hope God blesses your lives. I thank Jesus for bringing all of you into my life."

I ran to put on my apron and take orders. As I saw each of my friends leave I'd give them a hug and say good-bye. I never saw any of them again.

Settling at Salt Lake City, Utah

That night I drove to Grandma's house and talked to Freda May about moving to Salt Lake City, Utah. "My truck driver friends think it's the safest city for two single girls," I said.

Freda May didn't care where we lived. To her, Salt Lake City was as good as any other city. I moved everything except clothing to Grandma's house. She said she would keep my piano until I could move it later. The lady who was my landlord at the trailer park was nice about it. Right on schedule I was on my way to Grandma Brown's house where Freda May and I stayed until it was time to leave. I phoned a truck stop in Salt Lake City and lined up a job for me.

Freda May had a midsize car with a six-cylinder engine; I had a compact car with a four-cylinder engine. We packed all our clothes and miscellaneous belongings and headed for Salt Lake City the next day.

Storms in Wyoming nearly blew us off the road. By the time we got to Salt Lake City we were exhausted. At our hotel we slept in the next day. Then we moved into an apartment on the north side of Salt Lake City near the capitol building. Freda May found a factory job as a power sewing machine operator a few weeks later.

We phoned Grandma nearly every week. She told Freda May she could have her mobile home, so my sister made arrangements several months later to have it moved. Anna Kate had been living in Freda May's trailer. Out of the blue came Freda May's call that she had made arrangements to move the trailer in three days. Quickly Anna Kate looked for another place to live. Anna Kate resented moving tremendously. The father of Roger's friend Mike owned some inexpensive duplexes. One happened to be empty at the time, so he let Anna Kate rent it for the monthly fee of sixty-five dollars. It had one bedroom, one bath, and a kitchenette. It was small but adequate.

Life in Utah

Freda May and I began to enjoy Utah's capital city. Loneliness plagued us at first. We missed Grandma so much. But we made friends and adjusted well to big-city life. Before long we joined a bowling league to play on Sunday evenings. Seven months after our arrival, Grandma's mobile home arrived. We rented a lot in a mobile home park, had the coach hooked up to sewer lines and water service, and moved in. In the soil in the back of the mobile home, I soon had a garden growing. The soil was terribly hard and fallow, needing mulch, special soil mixes, and fertilizer.

I was grateful for all that Jesus had done, but I decided to take control of my own life and leave Jesus in the background. In the fall of 1971, I decided to enter college to become a pilot. I was determined I would become the best pilot ever and no other profession would do. The general classes I took went fine. Then I climbed into a trainer for some classes aloft. Unfortunately, I found out quickly that I threw up every time I flew in an airplane. Stalling the airplane was terrifying. I kept thinking I could get past my fear of heights in a few months. The fear of heights continued for the next six months as well as the throwing up every time I got into the plane. During this time, I met a man walking in the park one weekend. He asked me out to dinner. I asked him if he was married. He said no, so we starting dating. I was so determined to be a pilot and stubborn that I would not even think of doing anything else. Finally, after eight months, the instructor told me that at best I'd become an average pilot. Most likely I would be a poor pilot. He told me I should consider learning how to something else that I was naturally good. I was devastated. I went home. When I walked through the door, Freda may told me she thought I was dating a married man. I said, "No way! I asked him and he said no."

Freda May said, "I think he is a liar. Ask him to take you to his home to see it. I bet he can't because he has a wife there."

I told her, "I'm going to prove you wrong!" I was to go to a concert in the park with him that afternoon. When he got to the door, I asked him to take me to his home. He hesitated. I realized that he was married and said, "You are married!"

He said, "I am getting a divorce."

I said, "Don't ever call me again! Your poor wife has been sitting home alone while you have been seeking the affections of another woman. It makes me want to puke! Marriage should be honored by all. Read Hebrews thirteen. You made a covenant with God. Don't you ever call me again!" I opened the door for him to leave. I never answered his calls again.

I didn't know how to run my life. Freda May had watched me make a mess of my life and told me I was a bigger mess than back in Kansas. I was so devastated about dating a married man that I felt maggots were all over me. I had picked the wrong man and the wrong profession. I looked at Freda May and said, "That does it! I'm not running my life anymore. I don't know what I'm doing. Jesus, the reins are all Yours. I'm sorry! I should have respected You to run it all along. Guide me in everything and make me the woman You want me to be. Amen." Freda May suggested that I see a counselor at the college to get an idea of I might be naturally good at. I set an appointment the next week.

The counselor asked me if I knew of any particular strength about myself.

I said, "No, none at all."

The counselor said, "Hmm, did you get any awards in high school?

"Perfect attendance and the bookkeeping award for all four years," I replied.

The counselor asked, "You got the bookkeeping award as a freshman? Isn't that unusual?"

I said, "I don't know; I didn't really think about it."

The counselor said, "I want to test you in math and reasoning skills."

I took three tests. On the appointment the following week, I got the news that I scored well on all three tests with the math score the highest. The counselor told me I would do very well in accounting or finance. I thanked her and felt good that Jesus was directing me to a profession that I was naturally good. "Thank You so much, Jesus!" I exclaimed when I got home, dancing around the room.

Born Again

Freda May made friends with some college kids at the University of Utah Campus Crusade for Christ. My sister accepted Jesus as her Savior and began to read the Bible daily. When she told me about it, I was thrilled, but I was also surprised because I thought she had made that decision many years earlier.

At one of the Campus Crusade for Christ meetings with Freda May, I met Mary Beth. We hit it off instantly. This spunky, genuine lady needed a roommate, so after considering her invitation I moved out of the mobile home with my sister and into the rooming house with Mary Beth. Monthly rent was only forty dollars. Space seemed cramped, and sometimes food became a hassle because many of the young ladies in the dorm helped themselves to my food in the refrigerator. "It's community food," they'd tell me with a straight face, never offering to replace what they'd take or pay for it.

Working two jobs kept me so busy that I was able to see my sister only about once a week. When Mary Beth invited me to travel with her to Denver to see a girlfriend, I readily agreed. I managed to get a three-day weekend, so off we went to meet the old friend.

She seemed nice but confused. To her, getting drunk was the greatest. Attending parties was her favorite pastime. "That's what I call living," she said, but Mary Beth and I said nothing. We bought her some groceries, prayed for her, and left.

In the Colorado capital I looked to the east where the vast farmlands made me homesick for Kansas. To the west, those majestic mountains rose like sentinels to bless and inspire. Coloradans made me feel at home. Back home in Salt Lake City, Anna Kate phoned with the news that she and Roger were getting married. During Anna Kate's last two years of high school she enrolled in a beauty college, which was like a trade school specializing in cosmetology. Incredibly, the school had a "work your way through college" program requiring two years of afternoons and Saturdays. My sister paid only fifty dollars for a kit at the beginning of the course. With barely enough money for gas, rent, and food, she stuck with it. At 6:00 p.m. each evening and on weekends she worked as a busgirl in a steak restaurant until 11:00 p.m. Needless to say, Anna Kate did not have a normal teenage life. By the time she graduated from high school she also was able to graduate from beauty college and was married a few days afterward.

In Salt Lake City, Freda May and I joined a small Protestant church and prayed for direction and strength. Several of my credit cards were charged to the max to buy clothing. Once when my car broke down, I had no credit left for repairs, so I borrowed the money from Freda May. I vowed that day that I would quit buying things on credit until I could pay off every dime charged on those cards.

There were such nice people in Salt Lake City, but I never felt at home. I became determined to move. I called Grandma and asked her, "Do you think I should move to Kansas City or to Denver?"

"Don't move to Kansas City," she said, "or your mother will interfere in your life. Move to Denver so you can stay closer to Freda May."

Freda May preferred that I stay in Salt Lake City because I knew no one in the Colorado capital. "Mary Jo," she counseled, "you don't have one friend in Denver and don't even know anyone."

"God will bring me friends," I replied. "He always brings me friends when I need them."

Freda May eventually gave up trying to talk me out of the move. She decided to return to college and earn her degree, sold the mobile home to cut her expenses in half, and rented a room in the home of new friends. When I visited her a week later in her new place, she and her host couple sat me down and talked to me about where I would live in Denver.

"I need to keep my overhead low because I want to save up for college," I told them.

My sister gave me eight hundred dollars, half the money from the sale of her mobile home. She didn't have to do it. Her mobile home was a gift from Grandma to her. She didn't need to give me anything. Her new hosts owned a small eight-by-thirty-foot mobile home they offered to sell for one thousand dollars. I had the extra two hundred dollars, but I looked the place over thoroughly. It would need a new furnace, but otherwise it was sound. The couple had a sister in Denver who knew of a small mobile home park on Federal Boulevard where I could pay fifty dollars a month lot rent. That was the lowest overhead I could possibly hope for. Everything was set.

Leaving my eldest sister was hard. I had brought her to Salt Lake City; now I was leaving her. She liked her job too much to want to move with me. I promised to visit her at least once a year and kept my word. Now Freda May lives in Denver so I can see her as much as I want. Yay!

Anna Kate Says "I Don't"

During this year, life for our youngest sibling was hard. She had no guidance or parental help. Life's biggest decisions (marriage, work, and friendships) she made alone. She decided she did not love Roger anymore. She became convinced that she had missed out on her early years because of her marriage, so she traveled back to Missouri to see Mom, struggling to make a decision about straightening out her life. Mom could give her little help because her own marriage and finances were so messed up. Three days with Mom was enough. She returned to Oklahoma, decided to get a divorce from Roger, and see what life was like as a single woman.

I phoned Anna Kate and asked my sister, "Are you sure you know what you're doing? Roger's a nice man. I know he loves you."

"I'm not staying married to Roger, period," she told me. "What do you know about love, Mary Jo?"

"Not much," I admitted, "so I'm avoiding it like the plague. But I'm simply telling you, Jesus expects you to keep your vows and stay married. God hates divorce."

"I know, but I can't stay married. I didn't know what I was doing." It was too late. Anna Kate had put into gear the paperwork to split from her youthful husband. I wished my sister had waited to be married. She hurt Roger badly because he didn't know what he had done wrong and really loved her.

Chapter 7

COLORFUL COLORADO

He fulfills the desires of those who fear him; he hears their cry and saves them. The Lord watches over all who love him, but all the wicked he will destroy.

—Psalms 145:19–20 (NIV)

Freda May's landlords hooked my trailer to their pickup and pulled it from Salt Lake City to Denver. I followed them all the way in my compact Escort and then watched the husband level my home and hook up the sewer and a temporary water hose. Fifty dollars a month rent plus utilities looked pretty good. This budget allowed me to pay my way through college. Working at a nearby restaurant gave me the extra book income I needed. Jesus also provided an accounting job so I could start to get some accounting experience. Life was sweet.

My Good Samaritan

A weakness of mine is a lack of mechanical dexterity. One Saturday, I got off work in the midafternoon and bought some copper tubing at a hardware store. Back at my trailer, I unhooked my water hose and tried to install the copper tubing to the waterline coming into my trailer.

As I struggled to make the thing work I said aloud to God, "I hate all this mechanical mumbo jumbo!"

A lady nearby laughed. "Are you having trouble over there?" she called.

"That's the understatement of the year," I said. "I'm trying to hook up copper tubing to the water spigot. I called a place and they want fifty bucks to do the job, can you believe that?"

My neighbor smiled. "I know how to hook up your copper tubing," she said. "I have the tool but not the strength to use it."

"I am very strong," I told her, "I just don't know what I'm doing with this stuff. My name's Mary Jo, what's yours?"

"Marie. My husband and I have just moved here from Fort Morgan, Colorado. You heard of that town?"

"No. I don't know any of the smaller towns in this state, but I'd love to visit sometime."

"I'm going to look for the tool," Marie said. "Be right back." I thanked her profusely and waited. About half an hour later she was back, showing me how to fit the copper tubing into a metal ring. Her tool curled the copper around a ring to seal it. Eager to try, I sat down in a chair beside the water line, took the tool, and set it in place. I used all my strength and saw the copper tubing curl beautifully into place.

"Wow," Marie exclaimed, looking closely. "I've seen a lot of men who couldn't curl the copper that good. You are strong!"

"Thanks," I replied. "It's come in handy a few times before. I sure appreciate your help." I took a good look at Marie. "What are you, a hundred pounds soaking wet?" I asked with a laugh. Marie smiled and said she weighed ninety-eight pounds. I looked at her and said, "I weighed that much when I was ten years old." We both laughed.

Marie advised me to wrap an electrical heat tape around my pipes so they wouldn't freeze that winter.

My neighbor invited me to her trailer for a drink. She had a little boy almost two years old. She was dating John, nearly seven years older, when she got pregnant. She married before she was eighteen with her father's permission. During the visit to her home I fell in love with Robert, her cute little son. Her husband was okay, but aloof. Little Robert got a grip on a crystal candy dish, so Marie tried to get it away from him. She slapped Robert's wrist to make him let it go. When her husband saw that, he smacked Marie so hard she was propelled across the room. I could not believe my eyes.

"You'd better not hit her again when I'm here," I told him, frowning. "If you do, I'll use every ounce of my strength to take you down. I don't even care if I win. I can make sure you know how it feels to be beat up."

I left and slammed the front door, disgusted by my neighbor's act of unkindness. "God," I prayed that night, "please give me the strength to avoid any temptation to have a man in my life. I don't tell you this everyday, but I am grateful for my peaceful life." I learned later that John had a problem with booze.

"Why do you take those beatings?" I asked Marie.

"They aren't that often and besides, I love him."

"If that's love," I told her, "I'm going to pray extra hard tonight that I'll have the strength to avoid it like the plague."

Marie hung her head. "I married too young," she told me, "but I am committed—even for the very worst."

"Well, I admire you for that, Marie. Just know that Jesus loves you way too much to see you beat up all the time. I'll always be your friend, no matter what John does to you."

John began drinking more and the beatings increased.

My Needy Friends

I loved the accounting clerk job doing payables and receivables in an office and worked a second job on weekends to save money for college, but I made time for my neighbors. What an interesting bunch they were.

Peg next door, lived alone with his cat. After several months I adopted him officially as my father. I looked in on this elderly gent every day and watched his emphysema worsen as he puffed away on cigarettes.

"Are you going to stop someday?" I asked him.

"Mary Jo, I cannot quit," he told me. "I'll smoke until I die."

"Guess it's better not to start bad habits, eh?" I said.

"I agree, but it's too late for me." A few months later he began carrying his oxygen everywhere, smoking as he went despite the extreme danger of setting off an explosion.

Sharon, my best friend from Kansas, had been married a year earlier in Kansas. Now here they were, living next to me in our cramped quarters. Her husband was a nice-looking man, but he turned ugly to me when I learned how he treated his wife. They got into an argument about something. Next thing I knew she was banging on my door and calling out desperately.

I let her in just before her husband began yelling in high decibels outside my gate, threatening to beat her up and kill her. He called Sharon a "female dog name" and cursed at her loud enough for the entire trailer camp to hear.

I quickly phoned the police, who came in ten minutes. First they talked to the husband, then to Sharon. When her husband started threatening her again I stepped in. "Look," I said, "if you so much as touch her you'll have me to reckon with." The police separated us and told us both not to talk anymore. Sharon stayed the night with me, afraid to go home.

I phoned my elder sister, disgusted by what I had seen. "I just want you to know how much I hated my dad for beating me up over the years," I told Freda May. "Now my two best friends have husbands who beat them. Is this just bad luck? Or is there something really wrong with the male half of this world?"

"Now, Mary Jo," Freda May began, "you can't generalize about men. Every man is his own individual. You're just witnessing some bad actions by two of them. Next time it could be a woman. People get lost when they don't know Jesus. They can do horrible things to one another. I'm sorry you had to see all that. I'll bet you're more convinced than ever to stay from men!"

"You've got that right," I said. "If I ever decide to get married, I hear I'll have a one out of two chances that the marriage will work. Then coming from a broken home—that gives me a greater chance that the marriage will fail. On top of that, because I had an abusive father, I have a one in ten chance of the marriage working. Multiply all these together and I have a one in a hundred chance of my marriage working. Those are lousy odds."

"I've been praying for your future husband," said my big sis.

"You're scaring me," I told her. "How do you know I'd treat a husband right? Aren't you worried that I might make him pay for what Dad did to us?"

My sister calmed me with her reply: "I'm not worried. Jesus has given you too sweet a heart to be mean for long."

"You are the best sister anyone could ask for," I told her. "I appreciate your prayers. And I'll be praying that this man, if he exists, will not come into my life until I graduate from college. Preferably not before I'm forty or fifty years old."

"Mary Jo, remember," Freda May reminded me, "God is stronger than you, and His plan for your life will be done. If He wants you to be married, you'll be married."

"I can't pick a man," I commented. "If God wants me to marry someday He'll have to put him right in front of my face—and even then I'll look the other way. I will never voluntarily go down that road."

Freda May calmed my nerves. "God loves you so much. If He wants a husband for you, He will bring you one who treats you well and blesses your life. Remember: a husband is a gift from God."

"I know you're right," I admitted. "If God wants me to have a husband, I'll trust Him to pick a good one."

My sister and I encouraged each other every week. Each time I prayed that Jesus would keep me strong so no temptation would spoil my life. I thanked Him for the free time I enjoyed to help others and to watch and pray for His guidance for the next step.

Freda May enjoyed a good-paying job with a large company in Salt Lake City. Within a few months after my move to Denver she met a man and started dating. They decided six months later to be married. That meant my sister would have to quit college. "Finish college," I urged.

"Mary Jo, I don't want to go to college anymore. I'm going down a different road now. I want to have a family."

"Okay, if you're sure," I replied.

"I'm very sure."

Trailer Trials

Sharon and her husband kept fighting. They had one child when they divorced. Sharon's mother told me they both had problems with alcohol. Sharon lost custody of her child for a while because of her drinking.

"Mary Jo, you're always the stable one," Sharon's mother told me.

"I don't know about that," I replied. "I've had my problems. If I go through life without getting drunk, taking drugs, or fighting others, I'll give credit to God."

College at Last!

Two years after moving to Colorado, I had saved up more than two thousand dollars for my first year of college. Two weeks after registration opened, Marie discovered I still had not registered.

"I can't believe you weren't the first in line," my neighbor said, "and heaven help anyone who tried to stop you!"

"You know me well, friend," I said.

I seized an empty pop can on the table. "Yes, I am so strong," I said, smashing the can flat. Then I looked up at Marie. "But you know, I am also weak. My dream for many years has been to go to college, do well, and graduate. Now I'm afraid I'll fail. I'm pretty weak, huh?"

Marie stooped over and gave me a big hug. "Mary Jo, I know you are smart and will do well in college. If something's hard, you'll just study twice as long. Now let me tell you what to do: sign up for that first class. Don't tell me or anyone that you've signed up. This will be just between you and God. When you pass that first class, sign up for two more. Next thing you know, you'll be graduating from college."

I signed up for college that day—a class in general business procedures. Two days a week. I did my homework on the other nights, focusing like a laser on my work, getting organized, and getting my homework done. Praying before every test for wisdom. Two weeks later Marie knocked on my door one evening. She said, "Where have you been keeping yourself?" She noticed the college book and supplies but said nothing.

"I've been busy," I said. I pulled out my first test and showed her a score of eighty-nine—one point from an A. Marie had helped me get through an insecurity that had plagued me for years. Meeting her was no accident. She became my best friend. I spent every holiday with her and her family. We shopped together and played with little Robert together. When I chased my little friend we laughed so loudly that Marie would make us play outside. Marie's dad would come to Marie's house for the holidays. He treated me like a second daughter. What fun we had over those few golden years in the trailer park.

Unfortunately, John's drinking became heavier, and his health become worse. So did the physical abuse he gave to his faithful wife. With all of this going on in my neighborhood I focused on my studies all the more. I began taking three and four classes while working full time. I started at Community College of Denver (now Front Range College) and got an associate of art degree. Then I was working toward a bachelor of science degree in accounting at Metropolitan State College (now Metropolitan State University).

In order to speed up graduating, I started to take nine to twelve semester hours each semester. This meant three to four classes of homework in addition to full-time employment. Many nights I worked until 2:00 a.m. to finish homework. I went to school right through the summer, taking up to three classes to make up for the classes I couldn't take in the spring or fall. One semester I took fifteen credit hours while working full time. It was so hard that I decided not to do that again. On holidays I worked at the truck stop to have money to buy textbooks.

With this schedule I was never lonely. I talked to my sisters once a week. Anna Kate decided to move to Alabama with her new boyfriend. Freda May became a mother of two children and decided to be a stay-at-home mom.

My first two and a half years of college did not deplete my savings because the Colorado scholarship paid for my tuition as long as I kept a 3.5 GPA. At Metropolitan State College; that scholarship was available only to the top accounting student. As a result, college tuition started depleting my savings.

In my second year of college, I met Dave in speech class. Though he was quiet, we had a lot of fun in the class. Our teacher had a booming personality and got us all involved in every speech.

On the last day of class, Dave asked for my telephone number. He phoned the following weekend and invited me to a movie. We started going out every Saturday night. But after a couple of months, he took me to a friend's house where I noticed an odd smell. Guests were sitting in a circle talking and inhaling something in a funny-shaped plastic container.

"What's going on?" I asked Dave.

"My friends are just getting high after a hard week's work," he explained. "Would you like to try it?"

"No, thanks," I replied.

Dave looked at me funny. "Brian's wife here (pointing to Laura) doesn't get high either. I don't know how she resists. It's so nice to get high and not have a worry in the world."

I watched people getting high that night and noted how it changed them. What were those drugs doing to their brains? Dave finally took me home.

The next day I asked my neighbor, Peg, about the evening. "Mary Jo," he warned, "if you want to finish college, you can't be up there. No tellin' what that stuff does to the brain."

"That's just what I was thinking," I said. "You know, we must be a lot alike. Maybe that's why we get along so well. I'm going to tell Dave it's best we don't see each other."

Harvesting Hope

"Good idea," Peg said. "You can always spend Saturday nights with me if you get lonely."

I thanked him and gave him a big hug. Now I just needed to tell Dave.

When he phoned the following week asking if I wanted to go to Brian's place, I declined. "Why don't you come to my house for a change?" I suggested. "I'll fix you dinner."

At six o'clock he knocked on my door. Dinner was ready—pork chops, mashed potatoes and gravy, and green beans. I told him how my classes were going. When the meal was finished he asked, "Why didn't you want to go to Brian's tonight?"

"I don't feel comfortable there," I explained. "I don't like seeing people shoot up and snort drugs."

Dave shook his head. "Mary Jo, you go high in the sky without a worry in the world."

"You don't get it, Dave. That's just an illusion. You have more worries taking that stuff. No telling how much it's messing up your brain."

"You don't get it," he shot back. "I was planning on us getting married if you will come with me and get high."

I reflected on the offer. "Dave, I am not going up there. I can get high down here with Jesus and feel good just from hard work and enjoying my family and friends. Going up there means turning my back on everyone who loves me down here. You may be letting someone down by getting high in the sky—someone who needs your help."

"I can't believe you'd give up our marriage and not come with me."

"I'm staying down here," I said emphatically. "I cannot do anything up there. I am determined to make a difference for Jesus, and I need all the brains He gave me. I wish you the best, Dave. Good-bye."

I kept on working and going to college, drawing strength from my Jesus.

Mary Jo Brown

A Day in the Life of ...

My days in the trailer park fell into a predictable routine. I awoke at 7:00 a.m., dressed for work, and arrived at 8:00 a.m. I worked until 5:00 p.m. My first class at college started at 6:00 p.m. My last class ended at 9:20 p.m.

Classes were held four days a week, Monday through Thursday. Afterward I would feed my German shepherd-collie mix named Charley Boy. My pet was the sweetest dog on earth—and smart too. I would play with him for a few minutes and then dive into my studies.

At around 11:00 p.m. I'd become sleepy. Knowing I had two or three more hours of homework, I'd celebrate the peaceful life that God gave me by playing my celebration song on an old record player.

"I don't tell you every day, thank You for my peaceful life," I'd sing as I danced, did my aerobics, and jumped around for twenty minutes. It was so much fun that Charley would sit and stare at me as though I were a wild woman. I would laugh, give him a big hug, and pet him for a few minutes. Then I'd return to my studies. Often it would take me until 3:00 a.m. to finish, but usually I was finished by 2:00 a.m. Charley, my watch dog charged with the responsibility of keeping me awake, would be asleep by then.

Seven a.m. came early. Sometimes I had a hard time getting up. On weekends I slept in, did all my extra homework projects, and prepared notes for tests. Between semesters I'd work at the truck stop for money to pay for the next semester's books. I husbanded every nickel, but every semester's tuition slowly drained my savings.

Wedding Bells for Freda May

In 1975, Freda May started dating a man who proposed marriage and she accepted. I played the organ at her wedding. She seemed to be supremely happy. Later she became a stay at home mom with two children.

In the bride's room, as we were preparing for the wedding, my sister and I noticed a white strand in my carefully coiffured hair.

"Boy, that is really light blond hair you have there," Freda May exclaimed.

We both looked closely. "That's not blonde," I corrected. "That's a white hair, and I'm only twenty-three!" I quickly pulled it out.

Freda May laughed. "Two more will grow there, you know!"

"Maybe tomorrow, but not today," I corrected. Since then I have grown many white hairs—too many to pull out.

During the next January, I took one class in a one-month session called Interim. I was one semester away from graduating with a bachelor of science degree. In my final semester, I was taking two accounting classes. Graduation was only a prayer away.

Que Sera ...

During those five years in college dramatic things happened to my best friends. Marie's husband had become so abusive that he was beating up his wife nearly every week. Marie would escape to my house for refuge, and John would pick her up the next day. Peg's emphysema worsened, but he could not quit dragging on the cigarette. His plight made me thankful that I had never started that bad habit. Mary Beth in Salt Lake City struggled with her career plans and felt more uncomfortable there. She decided to move to Denver. Anna Kate dated a man for about a year and then was married. She and her husband moved to Alabama where her husband's family lived. Three years later they had a baby girl. After another three years, her husband decided he needed other women in his life and started running around on her. Not long afterward they were divorced. Anna Kate had a terrible time adjusting to this situation. Raising a daughter as a single parent is never easy, especially when the father does not want to pay child support. The situation deteriorated so badly that life was a constant struggle.

Graduation Weekend

My final semester offered a light load, so I joined a single square dance club called the Fiddle Steppers. I love to square dance and thought it would be great fun. I met a lot of new friends there and regularly went one evening a week after classes. I made sure everyone knew that I was only looking for friends, not dates. Back at school during my final semester I saw Dave in the hallway. He looked the same. "How are you doing?" I asked.

"Real good," he replied. "How far have you gotten in college?"

"I'm graduating this May," I said. "Almost done. How close are you to graduating?"

"When I finish this class, I will be classified as a sophomore."

"That's good. Stay with it. I wish you the best." I have never seen Dave since that day. I don't know if he graduated or not.

Before graduating, I had an opportunity to purchase a larger mobile home. It was a good deal. Mary Beth decided to move to Denver and become my roommate. She and Marie planned a graduation party for me.

For those final two weeks I studied hard, burning the midnight oil so I could graduate with at least a B average. I was beginning to grow weary of school because it had been five years since I started. Even though it was a demanding commitment, it was worth every minute. After graduation the following week, Mary Beth and Marie would meet me at graduation and afterward we would go out to dinner and celebrate. I graduated with a Bachelor of Science degree with no help except from Jesus. He had given me the wisdom and health to reach my goal. After my final test I was exhilarated. I had stayed the course.

Peg told me he was proud and happy for me and that he couldn't be prouder of me, his own daughter.

The graduation was huge because so many were graduating. After the graduation was over, I spotted Mary Beth and Marie in the crowd, slipped up the aisle, and motioned for them to come with me. They followed me outside the room. So we went out to eat and celebrate. It was so much fun! We danced the night away to rock and roll music. It ended up being almost an all-night celebration. I am so grateful for both of them. I went back to Kansas a few weeks later and showed Grandma Brown my diploma and tassels. Grandma was so happy.

"Jesus looked at them and said, 'With man this is impossible, but with God all things are possible'" (Matthew 19:26).

I am amazed by the work of His hands. His great love is precious to me. Jesus loves you too!

I began planning my life in the following weeks after college, praying hard for direction. I longed to help others, but what would I do? I asked my pastor what ministry he would suggest. He listed fifteen or twenty to choose from. Soon I had so many ideas that I would have to live three lifetimes to do everything I wanted to do.

Chapter 8

WHAT I AM DOING NOW?

And the Lord said, "Who is that faithful and wise steward, whom his master will make ruler over his household to give them their portion of food in due season? Blessed is that servant whom his master will find so doing when he comes.

—Luke 12:42-43

I am working full-time as an accountant. I love detail work, so it's a good fit.

I joined a ministry that goes into the Denver jail and the Adams County jail giving Bible studies and testifying to God's great mercy and love. It is amazing to me how I can go back home to Kansas and clean my dad's floor and feel nothing—no anger, grudge, or revenge feelings. My dad is totally forgiven. That is a reason to praise Jesus because if you read this book, you already know that I used to hate his lousy guts.

I also love to go to halfway houses and encourage the women to live a godly life. We study the Bible to learn what a godly woman does. We talk about addictions and temptations also.

I'll serve in anything that Jesus opens the doors to. I pray that I can be more like Jesus so I can live a life pleasing to Him. I pray the same for you. I pray that we can be walking in truth because Jesus is able to keep us from stumbling and will present us faultless with exceeding joy to the Father (Jude 24).

It doesn't get any better than that in my opinion. I am so looking forward to that, but in the meantime, I will be about my Father's business.

EPILOGUE

Uncle Bill (Mom's brother)

It took me years to find out what happened to Uncle Bill and Uncle Carl after Mom left. They lived out of a car for months until one of their older sisters took them in. Their teenage years were not easy. Uncle Bill lives in Nebraska and has five children. Uncle Bill and his wife are still living in the same small town in Nebraska.

Uncle Carl (Mom's youngest brother and youngest of the eight siblings)

Uncle Carl's dad died when he was nine. After living in a car for months with Uncle Bill, Uncle Carl lived with an older sister for years. At eighteen, Uncle Carl married and then got drafted to Vietnam. He got malaria over there and nearly died. He came back to Kansas and enjoyed life with his wife. They had three children. When his oldest child, a boy, turned nine, Uncle Carl told his son how he had lost his dad at nine and how it had devastated him. He told his son to be grateful he had a dad to be part of his life. Two weeks later driving home from work, a gasoline truck with a driver who was drinking ran a stop sign and plowed into Uncle Carl's pickup, killing him instantly. Uncle Carl was only thirty-three years old. He is the only person I can remember in my family to die young. It was devastating!

Grandma Patterson (Mom's mom)

I never understood her at all. I didn't understand why Uncle Bill and Uncle Carl couldn't go to their mother when Mom left Dad. I never understood why Grandma Patterson complained about all her kids except for Uncle Carl. She seemed miserable, and the only thing that made her happy was complaining. When Uncle Carl died, Grandma Patterson said she had no reason to live and wanted to die. I asked her, "Why can't you live for Jesus and to see your other children and Uncle Carl's children?"

Grandma Patterson said, "No. I was only living for Carl."

Six months later, Grandma Patterson was dead. It was all hush, hush, but rumor had it that Grandma Patterson got a cold and went to the hospital. She did not tell the hospital that she was allergic to penicillin, and the hospital gave her penicillin. Grandma Patterson had an allergic reaction and died. I went to her funeral and asked all my aunts and uncles if they knew what had happened, but nobody knew for sure. I hope she went to heaven to be with Jesus.

Mom

Mom and my stepdad were alcoholics. When I visited them after high school, I would open up the fridge and find nothing in it but alcohol. My stepdad said that he was leaving to go to the lake nearby to fish and that if he couldn't catch any fish, they would starve. They moved from state to state one step ahead of the bad checks they wrote. Most of our adult years, the four of us did not know where they lived or how to get a hold of them. The addiction took a toll on their bodies and both died years ago.

Marie

Marie has stayed one of my best friends through the years. She got a divorce when the beatings got too tough from her first husband. Marie married a nice, gentle man a few years later. They live in

Omaha, Nebraska, now. We visit each other practically every year. I appreciate her friendship so much!

Mary Beth

Mary Beth also has stayed one of my best friends through the years. Mary Beth moved to Upstate New York. Mary Beth works hard at a university and guess what—she worked hard for four years and got her master's while in her fifties! She even did that while working full-time! She had to write a thesis that put me in awe of her writing skills. Mary Beth has been an inspiration to me. She has taught me that it's never too late to improve. I am very grateful for our friendship!

Sharon

Sharon still lives in a small town in Kansas that is close to where we grew up. I see her every time I visit in Kansas. I haven't forgotten all the wonderful things she did when I was growing up! Sharon was working as a licensed practical nurse when she damaged her shoulder lifting a patient. She is in constant pain and has had several surgeries. She needs another surgery now. I will always be grateful that Jesus brought her into my life.

Uncle Hank Ray (Dad's brother)

Uncle Hank Ray kept on drinking and fighting with neighbors. He ended up in jail many more times asking Grandma to sell more land because he needed the money. Grandma never could say no and gave him money every time he asked. Some of the townsfolk said that they saw Uncle Hank Ray take Grandma Brown by the hair across the street to the bank to get more money. Uncle Hank Ray developed esophageal cancer and died a couple of years after Grandma Brown.

Dad

Dad is ninety-three years old and driving to town every Friday to get groceries. Dad looked for another wife after Zelda died but never found one. Dad made a mistake twenty years ago by selling the farm except for six acres instead of giving the farm to Bobby Dean. Dad had promised the farm to Bobby Dean since he had worked the farm for no money since he was six. Dad sold the farm within a year after Zelda died and did not tell anyone. The new owner was fixing a tube in a ditch when Bobby Dean asked him what he was doing. The new owner said, "I am fixing the tube. I bought the land a year ago." Bobby Dean could not believe it at first. He confronted Dad, and Dad admitted it. Bobby Dean was so hurt. He told Dad that he was no better than his brother selling off all the land. Bobby Dean felt betrayed. It took him several years to forgive Dad. Dad regrets that decision and wishes he could have the farm back. Dad reads the mail every day for most of his waking hours. He rarely sees anyone. I have compassion for Dad. It nearly killed him to have Mom leave. Everything he did is forgiven. Jesus forgave us all, for all have sinned. No one is righteous, no not one.

Zelda

While I was in college in Colorado, Zelda developed some kind of abdominal cancer. In the middle of a semester in my third year of college, Bobby Dean called and told me that her cancer was fatal and that the doctors were using her as a guinea pig to try out different drugs. Zelda died a few months later. Zelda did not inherit the farm as she had boasted for years before. God is in control and determines how long we are down here on earth. Zelda was the first to die in Kansas. I am grateful to Zelda that she made me need help to survive. Because of Zelda, I accepted Jesus as my Savior. It was the best decision I've ever made! And yes, Zelda is totally forgiven, and I hope she repented, accepted Jesus as her Savior, and went to heaven to be with Jesus forever.

Grandma Brown

Grandma Brown stayed in Kansas for the rest of her life, never going back to Oklahoma. Grandma lived to be one month shy of 102 years old. Grandma Brown bailed Uncle Hank Ray out of jail so many times.

Grandma was a loving woman. Even when we were angry or depressed about Mom, Dad, or anything else, she kept on loving us. Grandma disliked conflict and had a hard time saying no to anyone. I will be forever grateful for Grandma. She gave us love when others didn't. She took us into her home when our mother abandoned us and our dad couldn't take care of us. Praise Jesus that He made sure we had the right grandmother to love us unconditionally! Grandma led me to Jesus Christ, and I am so glad! I believe with everything I am that I would not be alive today without Jesus. Grandma was right; I would have given in to the hate without Jesus.

Freda May

Freda May lived in Utah for many years and then moved to Colorado about ten years ago. It is so nice to get together with her and her husband. Freda May told me the other day that no one will be able to separate us again. I pray to Jesus that my almighty God would stop another separation. My God is a faithful God that loves us and hears our prayers. My sister and I can see each other any day we wish. Yay!

Freda May is an excellent seamstress. She makes mittens for the homeless, quilts for the sick in hospitals, and bags to carry food at the food banks as well as serving in the church. We pray that we are servants that are pleasing to Jesus and that we always stay humble.

Anna Kate

Anna Kate moved to Alabama after living in Oklahoma for five or six years. After Anna Kate got established in Alabama, she purchased a building and started her own beauty shop. She is very good.

Anna is still gorgeous today. She spends practically every Saturday with her granddaughter. Anna Kate loves to go on walks and four-wheeling.

And yes, Anna Kate has twenty pairs of underwear, and so do I. I call that another "Praise Jesus."

Bobby Dean

Bobby Dean lives up the hill west of the small town in Kansas that we grew up in. He farms our grandmother's one piece of land that is in a trust. My brother also farms some other neighbor farms. My brother bought a sixty-five-acre farm next to Grandma's a few years back. I am so happy for him. He broke the trend of our family members selling off land. My brother works very hard farming, hauling grain to the elevator, bulldozing, and excavating. My brother is respected around the community. He helps friends and neighbors in times of need. I enjoy going four-wheeling around the farm and countryside with my brother, something I cannot do in the city. I always enjoy going back to Kansas to visit so much! In my opinion, Kansas folk are some of the finest people on the face of the earth!

Mary Jo (me)

I am so grateful that I have such an awesome God that not only has an exquisite love for us, but is our fortress, our shelter, our provider, our healer, the director of our paths in life, and our strength when temptation or the pain of loss comes our way.

The love of Jesus is precious! I'll admit this to you: I used to feel that I was unlovable when Mom left and Dad couldn't take care of us. I have seen so much unlove, how people divorce each other, how they abandon their friends, children, or other family. It makes a love like Jesus's so precious! Jesus says in Hebrews 13:5, "I will never leave you and I will never forsake you." That means so much to me. Just know that everyone in this book that hurt me is forgiven. Forgiving them took away my anger, and it felt like a thousand pounds off my shoulders. In Matthew 6:14–15, it says "If you forgive others the wrongs they have done to you, your Father in heaven will also forgive you. But if you do not forgive others, then your Father will not forgive the trespasses you have done." I want forgiven for my sins and for my part of hurting anyone else. And yes, accepting Jesus Christ as my Savior was the best decision I ever made. Beloved by Jesus, what about you?

ABOUT THE AUTHOR

I still live in Colorado and love it. I currently live with my two sons. They are helping me, and I am helping them. We have a dog that is a black Shar-Pei. Her name is Jasmine. We have loved her so much that she will stand or sit and just take it. (I don't think she has any choice but to take it!) I take her walking every day. We both need the exercise. My sister and I sew gloves for the homeless and get them to the Denver Rescue Mission every fall. I sew other items and make outfits as well as repair them. I also play the piano. I love to sing and dance. I also love gardening and yard work. It is such an honor to go into the jails and prisons telling the inmates about Jesus. It amazes me how good the devil is at wrecking lives. But Jesus has overcome the world and says not to be afraid. We just need to stay in His love. I believe Jesus is the one true God. He has blessed my life and brought me a love for others that amazes me today. I wouldn't be alive today except for Jesus answering my prayers to protect me.

It's my prayer that this book will bring you to the Savior. If so, then I have truly made a difference here on earth. In the gospel of John 14:6 (NIV) Jesus told His disciples, "I am the way and the truth and the life. No one comes to the Father except through me."

Ephesians 2:10 (NIV) teaches: "We are God's workmanship, created in Christ Jesus to do good works, which God prepared in advance for us to do."

In Philippians 1:27–28 (NIV) the apostle Paul admonishes us: "Whatever happens, conduct yourselves in a manner worthy of the Gospel of Christ. Then whether I come and see you or only hear about you in my absence, I will know that you stand firm in one spirit, contending as one man for the faith of the Gospel without being frightened in any way by those who oppose you. This is a sign to them that they will be destroyed, but that you will be saved—and that by God."

I pray that you come to know Jesus so you can experience His great love that is beyond belief and allow Him to be a comfort to you like He has been for me. I hope that you honor Jesus in everything you do and that Jesus blesses you in everything you do and shines His face upon you!

Printed in the United States
By Bookmasters